The Past Matters

A Chronology of African Americans in The United Methodist Church

Marilyn Magee Talbert

Dedicated to the Past—
the ancestors and waymakers who made the journey
and left markers along the way for the rest of us;
and
To the Future—
the Magee and Talbert grandchildren,
their generation and generations to follow.
May they develop and continue to have a thirst
for learning, including learning about their heritage—
spiritually, culturally, and historically;
and
To my beloved, Melvin George Talbert,
without whose encouragement, patience, and
household management during long periods of research
and writing this work might not have been completed.

The Magee Grandchildren:
Sydney Layne Magee
Paige Elizabeth Magee
Joseph David Magee, IV

The Talbert Grandchildren:
Kaetlin Alexis Sifford
Melvin Douglas Sifford
James Howard Sifford, Jr.

Acknowledgments

For whatever its meaning and worth, this work could not have been produced without the support, encouragement, critique, and patience of a number of people. I appreciate the contributions made by those who have gone before me and who did so much for us with so little means and support. How unfortunate for us that so few records were maintained. Our beautiful legacy is the result of their selfless labor.

I express my gratitude for support and encouragement to

My dad, Richard Tyson, who gave me the heritage of Methodism and told me stories from the Bible as if he knew the characters;

My mother, Celesta Williams, who provided the day-to-day guidance and development of the Christian faith;

All the saints at Hartzell Memorial United Methodist Church in Chicago, who taught me, shaped my ministry, and allowed me to learn and develop my ministry with love and patience;

Nodie and Katherine Sampson, who nurtured me as a daughter;

My Clark family, especially all my Disciple Bible Study classes, my sisters in spirit, members of the choir, members of my Prayer Support Group, and others;

Black Staff Forum colleagues, past and current, a supportive and caring group whose dedication, intelligence, energy, and spirituality bring so much to the ministry they undertake day after day at the agencies, boards, and commissions of The United Methodist Church;

Donald Lusk of St. Mark United Methodist Church in Chicago, who was willing to share an important resource no longer in print;

The staff at the General Board of Discipleship, who were supportive of my work and with whom I have shared many learning experiences.

But most of all I am indebted to Linda Whited, editor, who believed in this project and guided me gently through the process of birthing this book.

Contents

Cover and book design by Nanci H. Lamar

Edited by Linda R. Whited, Cindy S. Harris, and David Whitworth

ISBN 0-88177-424-3

Library of Congress Control Number 2004112417

Scripture quotations, unless otherwise indicated, are from the New Revised Standard Version Bible, copyright 1989, Division of Christian Education of the National Council of the Churches of Christ in the United States of America. Used by permission. All rights reserved.

DR424

My Hopes for This Book

*Landmarks need to be sought out and recognized, and a new generation
deserves to be freed from the false bonds and misconceptions
of the past to move with understanding freedom into the future.*

(From *The Story of American Methodism*, by Frederick Norwood; © 1974 Abingdon Press.)

In 1984 as The United Methodist Church was moving toward the celebration of two hundred years of Methodism, I was serving as the Executive Director of Chicago Black Methodists for Church Renewal in the Northern Illinois Conference. This chronology was initiated for use in workshops and seminars. From time to time more information was added, yet no intensive research was undertaken. Recently a pastor who had been a young college student in 1984 called and asked about the timeline she recalled from a workshop. A search unearthed the material and rekindled the interest in chronicling the history of African Americans in The United Methodist Church.

African Americans have been a part of the woof and warp of Methodism since its inception. Yet far too many people in the denomination believe that African Americans (Blacks) came in large numbers only at the union of The Methodist Church and The Evangelical United Brethren Church in 1968. Time after time, I have been amazed at the lack of knowledge by both black and white United Methodists about African American heritage in The United Methodist Church and its predecessor bodies. As older generations begin to fade from the scene, the story must be retold afresh to a younger generation.

Many resources about "the black church" or even about Methodism give the impression that when Richard Allen, Absalom Jones, and James Varick left the Methodist Episcopal Church, all Blacks left with them. While many Blacks did leave the Methodist Episcopal Church, or were forced out, some of us are fourth- and fifth-generation Methodists, and thousands more have joined this church by choice. Significant achievements, accomplishments, and contributions have been made by these black constituents. And there are many more whose stories we do not know. Much of the research data follows those Blacks who left and reveals little about the thousands who stayed.

Just as important is the rich history that resides in collective memories or in family and church histories in each of the conferences. This book will have many gaps, but hopefully it will inspire people in every conference to seek out the histories of all the African American congregations and their people. Some have begun this work. Already some congregations have researched their history and have recorded it on the internet.

Methodism parallels the history of the United States, thus the story of African Americans in the church is the same as the story of the country in many ways. An examination of our history will show some of the parallels of racism in society and in the church. The parallels also show that the church has attempted to redress its wrong just as the secular society has done. Often the church has been just a step behind.

At the 1976 General Conference the missional priority "to strengthen the ethnic minority church" was established. Theoretically the missional priority designation meant that all of the denomination and its resources would go to the implementation and follow-through to achieve the identified goals of the priority. For the next four quadrennia, "developing and strengthening the ethnic local church" was the theme of the priority. To the credit of some of the boards and agencies, efforts were made through programming and offerings of training. Alas, however, the general church missed its opportunity to redress much of its neglect and the racism directed toward its ethnic populations. A number of conferences never developed conference plans, or established conference committees to address the priority, or even made lukewarm efforts to put the priority into effect.

Some conferences did develop comprehensive plans with specific strategies for helping ethnic churches develop and grow. Primarily, the major results seemed to be in individual leadership gains and the presence of ethnic people in various places where they had not been before. Ethnics (Blacks, Hispanics, Asians, and Native Americans) were discovered!

The 1992 General Conference directed the general boards and agencies to document their efforts over the past twenty years of helping to develop and strengthen ethnic churches. That report was received at the 1996 General Conference. Also presented and passed at that 1996 session was a proposal for "Strengthening the Black Church for the 21st Century." For the first time, a missional initiative was not centralized in a general agency but was centered in Congregation Resource Centers (teaching congregations). The Congregation Resource Centers provided teaching/training/mentoring to partner congregations. A coordinating committee named by the jurisdictional Colleges of Bishops and agency staff consultants provided governance for the initiative. The significance of this initiative was that it shared with the whole church that black churches within the denomination had something to share with one another and with the general church.

During the 2000 General Conference an "Acts of Repentance" service was held so that The United Methodist Church could "apologize" to the African Methodist Episcopal Church (AME), the African Methodist Episcopal Zion Church (AMEZ), and the Christian Methodist Episcopal Church (CME) for the role of the predecessors of The United Methodist Church in acts of racism that drove them from the Methodist Episcopal Church in the 1700's. Unfortunately, many Blacks who had descended from those who stayed in the Methodist Episcopal Church and those who had come to the denomination by choice were chagrined at this action. What is even sadder is that too many Whites in our denomination just didn't get it. They thought they were doing a great and magnanimous thing! But representatives of other denominations met the posture with some degree of skepticism. The representative from AMEZ Church stated, "We'll be watching you. We will be fruit inspectors." Will our behavior extend beyond a ceremonial program?

Prior to the Acts of Repentance worship service that night, a number of African Americans in The United Methodist Church agonized over the action they wanted to take. Some were angry. Some were frustrated. Most were just hurt. When had the church apologized to those who stayed? Were we not the ones who had endured the "sinful compromise" of 1939, when we had been the lambs of slaughter offered up to the segregationists? And had we not stayed? And had our foreparents not paid conference claims and supported institutions not open to us? Then there were the voices of those who did not want to rock the boat, saying we should simply accept the historical significance of the event.

In a late-night meeting the agreement was made to let people respond in the ways they were personally comfortable. Some African Americans decided not to attend. Some merely sat stonily throughout the service. Some refused to accept or wear the insignia distributed. Some wept tears of anger and frustration. And, unfortunately, there were those who did not even know what the fuss was all about!

We had nothing for which to apologize. And some of us were very hurt. It was yet another blow of humiliation from an insensitive and racist church yet unwilling to recognize its sisters and brothers among them.

Prior to the beginning of the worship service Rev. McAlister Hollins, pastor of the Ben Hill United Methodist Church in Atlanta, Georgia, who had been a member of the agency sponsoring the service, made a statement on behalf of the many African Americans who had remained in the denomination. Yet the service moved right along, with many feeling good about themselves and their ritual of repentance.

Such recent experiences sadly point out that The United Methodist Church has a story to tell. Unfortunately, too many of our white brothers and sisters fail to understand that our story is their story as well. We have always known their story. However, now we are faced with the reality that too many of our black sisters and brothers do not know our story.

The cultural and social lesson for us is like the story of the Christian faith. We must learn the story, tell the story, live the story, and celebrate the victory of faith embodied in the life, death, and resurrection of Jesus Christ. When one looks through the pages of history, one is amazed by the inner power and strength of our forebears of the faith. To them much gratitude, honor, and glory are due. They stayed faithful to God and to the Methodist Episcopal Church, learning and growing in the midst of all kinds of discrimination within the church. They took castoffs and made good things; they took the discarded and honed delicacies; and they made paths and roads where there were none. Indeed they traveled through Baca, leaving signs in the desert places for us to know where the hidden pools of water were located so that we would not die nor faint in desperate times (Psalm 84:5-7).

The following chronology is not the whole story, but it is offered as steps or landmarks along the journey. It is indeed a thumbnail sketch or a shorthand version of the story so that readers will be inspired to do the research themselves. I also hope that African Americans will begin to search out their stories in their annual conferences and local congregations and to write those stories. May new generations learn and be inspired to dig deeper into the history of a people who have come this far by faith leaning on the Lord, going on in faith to see what the end will be.

Too much of our history from early years has been lost. There are reasons, one of which is that African Americans were not allowed to learn to read and write. Oral skills had served the people well for centuries, and using them was most often a matter of survival since they were still the safest means of communication. As I have worked with the research materials, another reason I have discovered as to why things were often not written down is that making a living and making a life was the more important task. What was done in church and improvement of life seemed like natural works of mission. In later years writers have often been frustrated and discouraged by publishing arenas that did not believe there was an audience for their work.

I hope that this resource will be useful for leaders across the connection and our institutions. Leaders in congregations are encouraged to read with perceptive insight into how it can be used by confirmation and other educational groups, membership orientation, leader development, and other groups. It is also for reading by all African Americans with the hope that there is inspiration for telling their stories, writing their stories, and sharing with one another. There are many skilled and gifted people in our church who are making significant contributions and need to be heard. African Americans in each conference need to engage in research to unearth the legacy of treasures there.

This resource is not for African Americans only. It is for all of the members of The United Methodist Church, who need to know that their story has been missing some pages. Some will welcome the new knowledge, some may be embarrassed, and, regretfully, some will regard it lightly and consider it of no consequence. I am convinced, however, that there are many who will welcome the closing of the gaps in our corporate story.

My hope is that this resource will be used by individuals and groups desiring to learn and/or remember parts of the history that have not received a lot of interest. If this resource inspires others to study, research, and realize the significance of the past in forming and shaping the future, this book's purpose will have been accomplished.

In Search of Identity

own through the years, African Americans have struggled with issues of identity. In Africa people were Africans or were known by their tribal origins. Upon arrival on the shores of North America, Africans were identified by their color—*Negro*, which was Spanish for black. No other physical characteristics have defined one's boundaries of life as much as skin color even to this day. After Europe and America introduced the academic disciplines of anthropology and egyptology, the legitimacy of biological concepts of race and racial traits was launched. For almost two hundred years after they first set foot on American soil, people of African descent—even though they were second- and third-generation Americans—continued to accept the African identity.

Robert E. Hood refers in his book *Begrimed and Black* to "the church's unfinished symphony with blackness," as the church, too, used color as an excuse for the subordination of Blacks. In later years, the term *colored* was used as a more refined way of identifying people of African heritage. Blacks born in this country began to adopt the term *colored* in names of their social and political organizations. Early literature references are made to Negroes or Coloreds (Cullards). *Nigger* and *Nigga* were the derogatory names coined by white slave owners and continue to be used until this day, often by political leaders and others if they think they are talking off the record. Until recently, such terms were often used by African Americans with one another as a put-down expression. With the dawn of the music and hip-hop culture, young African Americans have used these terms in their music, demonstrating a lack of understanding about the emotion-laden experiences of their ancestors. Regardless of who uses the terms, the emotional scars of the meaning make them totally unacceptable for any usage!

During the civil rights struggles of the 1960's, many Blacks opted to be known as *Blacks*, a radical change for some who had chaffed at being called black in early years. As a matter of fact, to be called black had often been a fighting challenge. Older black people were comfortable with being called *Negroes*. Then with the rise of identifying people with their geocentric origins, the term *African American* came into usage. Some shortened this designation to *Afro-American*. Imagine how confusing for many white Americans (Euro-Americans) who were trying to be politically correct! Often when asked by white friends or colleagues about the proper usage to address me, I would respond by saying, "*Marilyn* will do."

Anthropological terminology uses color identity as red, white, black, yellow, or caucasoid, mongoloid. The issue is that all people have origins. For a long time in this country, though, racism created the image that all of Africa was a jungle of illiterate and ignorant people who had made no cultural contribution to the world. Blacks were reluctant to claim identification with the continent about which they knew so little. Education in this country was extremely limited or nonexistent about the great civilizations of Africa and about the contributions of Blacks in this country. In more recent years—as Black America has become more enlightened, as more scholarly work has been made available, and as writings by Blacks about Blacks have expanded—African Americans have become willing to reclaim the geocentric identification.

In addition to the cultural aspects of this chronology, it is important to note that this resource is also a chronicle of a people of faith. Long before reaching the shores of America, Blacks in Africa recognized and understood the meaning of divine encounters with the sacred and/or the divine. Africans viewed the entire universe as sacred. Rudolf Otto defines the encounter of humans with the divine as "*mysterium tremendum et fascinans*" (the mysterious, terrifying, and fascinating). Africans claimed and affirmed the great mystery as personal friend and as one readily available in and among the mundane struggles of daily life. Authors ascribe many practices of tribal descendents to African retentions. The retentions were used only in adaptations of the Christian faith that took the teachings that affirmed them as people of worth and children of God and discarded that which was used to deny their divine existence. Many black people have confessed their disregard of Paul because of the eisegetical teachings by slave owners and oppressors who read into the texts meanings that would justify their actions.

Yet the people of the diaspora were people of faith. In reviewing the journey, one never ceases to ask, How did they do it? What kept them strong in the faith? How do people of faith hang on in tough times when reviled simply because of skin color?

But faith it was that enabled our heroes and sheroes to provide a legacy to generations. One cannot read nor sing the words of spirituals and hymns created by oppressed people who found joy in the serving of Jesus Christ without feeling their faith. Many of these people came to faith without the benefit of organized religious worship. But they came out of conviction that they were children of God and that God would carry them through, that they would be lifted up and enabled to endure.

Our African Heritage

European enslavement of Africans began around the year 1300 when black Africans were among the slaves raising and harvesting sugarcane on the Mediterranean islands of Cyprus, Crete, and Sicily.

From the 1400's to the 1600's, Portugal dominated the slave industry. The practice was initiated by their expeditions of raiding Africa for slave exportation to Europe and the Americas. During this period a violent, ruthless, and profitable industry began; it would survive for more than four centuries.

African slaves were initially from up and down the west coast of Africa. Although the west coast remained the deportation place, some Africans were marched from inland regions to the coast. One of the deportation ports was on the Isle of Goree, which I have had the opportunity to visit. Goree, one of the last Dutch slave stations built, functions today as a museum. Yet this eerie fortress-type building seems to echo with the spirits of the past. It is a two-story structure, with several rooms or hovels on the ground level. The second floor has small hotel-type rooms where slave traders stayed and where they raped African women at will. On the lower floors were small cells called birthing rooms where women gave birth. Other cells were designated holding pens where young boys and men were held. Small dungeons, where it was impossible for a human to stand erect, were used as punishment rooms or to break the spirits of proud and defiant males, some warriors and some of tribal royalty. Iron rings and shackles still exist, embedded in the stone walls of Goree station.

There is a door from this fortress-type prison that is known as "the door of no return." It leads directly to the rocks and the sea below, where boats were waiting to carry the Africans to the large ships anchored further out in the sea. I found it an overwhelming and incredible experience to stand in this door and sense the spirits of the many ancestors who had been pushed through.

Estimates of the number of slaves exported from Africa range from eight million to twenty-five million. The numbers do not include those who died during the transatlantic voyage. While it is difficult to ascertain definitive numbers of the origins of many of the Africans, we do know that among the tribal representations included are the people called Ibo (Nigeria), Yoruba, Hausa, Fulani, and others. The voices and stories of millions of victims were never heard, yet their legacy of life to African Americans proves that the strong survive.

Our American Beginnings

*E*arly settlers in America were driven by several motives. Some came seeking freedom from the rule of the English Crown. Some were motivated by the ideals of a new government with input from its citizenry. Others came believing in the possibilities of wealth and the realization of dreams. And so they came, enduring the hardship of ocean passage and the harsh realities of harnessing new territories. Visions of freedom, liberty, and wealth made it all worth the efforts.

As they organized themselves into self-governing colonies, their foundations were shaped by the ideals and theologies of the Puritans and the Quakers.

England itself was emerging from the rebellion against the royalty and the Church State. It was moving toward the historic and famous English Bill of Rights, upon which our Bill of Rights would be patterned in 1791.

Almost from the beginning, the South was largely motivated by the possibilities of commerce and economics. There were the continuing ties with the commercial companies in

England. This dual and regional motivational concept set the stage for the differences that would ultimately cast the young nation and the church into a war of differences that lasted for centuries. To this day the differences are not fully reconciled.

American beginnings for Africans did not begin with slavery. Africans were hired to accompany a number of exploring expeditions, particularly with the Spaniards. Later, among the first settlers to arrive on American shores were Africans who were indentured servants rather than slaves.

THE FIFTEENTH CENTURY

1492 Christopher Columbus "discovered" America. Supported by Spain in his explorations, Columbus included African-Spaniard crew members, including one by the name of Pedro Alonzo Nino. Some sources identify the Blacks as "Negro." Negroes also accompanied other well-known explorers such as Balboa, Ponce De Leon, Cortes, Pizarro, and Menendez.

THE SIXTEENTH CENTURY

1538 Not all of the early explorers originated from Europe. Negro explorer Estevanico (Little Stephen) led an expedition from Mexico and discovered Arizona and New Mexico.

1541 Africans accompanied the explorer DeSoto as he surveyed the Mississippi River.

1542 The enslavement of Native Americans was outlawed by the Spanish monarchy. This measure increased the intensity of the African slave trade.

1565 During the 1500's, Africans were in sailing crews of explorers from Spain. A number of discoveries in the new world were made by Africans in those crews. One of those discoveries was St. Augustine, Florida. This area became the first home of free Africans and escaped slaves. St. Augustine, built by nonnative Americans, is one of the oldest permanent cities in the present-day United States.

SLAVERY IN AMERICA

Although this book chronicles African Americans in The United Methodist Church and its predecessor bodies, there is no escaping the profound impact of slavery on this nation, the role it had on the developing Methodist church, and the residual effect on all of the life of black people in this country. To put the issue of slavery in context, one has to go back before the settling of America. Slavery did not begin in the United States. As a matter of fact, it predated the legal existence of this country. It was not formally ended in England until 1833.

Nor, for that matter, did slavery end with the Civil War. After the emancipation, Blacks were to endure the humiliation of years of legal and defacto segregation, Jim Crowism, illegal hangings, and countless acts of terrorism often inflicted by officials sworn to uphold the law.

One's imagination does not have to stretch far to be able to see that the development of America, the institution of slavery and its residual results, and the development of Methodism were all inextricably interwoven. Perhaps the twenty-first century connotation of this nation is not a melting pot, maybe not even a salad, but a braided nation.

THE SEVENTEENTH CENTURY

1607 marks the beginning of the American colonies. From its beginning the new nation burned with the fire of freedom. The founders of the new nation did indeed bring forth "a new nation, conceived in Liberty, and dedicated to the proposition that all men are created equal" (Abraham Lincoln, The Gettysburg Address, 1863). This was the philosophy that led to the Revolutionary War in 1775 and brought forth new social, religious, political, and philosophical reverberations that have crossed the centuries of American life.

1619 One of the early groups of Africans to arrive on the shores of the new nation were not slaves but indentured servants. Indentured servants performed seven years of labor to a resident, after which they were to acquire their freedom. In that first group of twenty who arrived aboard a Dutch ship at Jamestown, Virginia, were Anthony, Isabella, Pedro, and seventeen others.

The indentured status was of short duration for Africans. It was not long before the first enslaved Africans began to arrive. Discovering the value of enslaved labor, Virginia began to build its agricultural economy on slave labor. Soon other southern colonies followed suit. This set the stage for the beginning of the "peculiar institution" known as slavery and the "race problem" that would permeate the nation and the church for three centuries.

1623 William Tucker, born in Jamestown, Virginia, is believed to be the first African child born in the North American colonies. The son of African indentured servants, William was baptized January 3, 1624.

1624 New Amsterdam (later to become New York) received enslaved Africans for the first time. They were brought by a Dutch slave ship.

1634 Massachusetts and Maryland received enslaved Africans for the first time.

1641 The first colony to legalize slavery was Massachusetts. Other colonies soon followed suit.

1644 Twenty years after arriving on New Amsterdam soil, eleven Africans successfully petitioned for their freedom.

1652 The first antislavery law enacted in the colonies was in Rhode Island. The law limited the term of servitude to ten years for both Blacks and Whites.

1663 From the beginning, the slaves rebelled against enslavement. For a number of years there were various plots to find a way back to Africa or to overthrow slavery by assault against slave owners. The first major conspiracy in the American colonies was discovered in Virginia in 1663.

1664 On September 20 Maryland enacted the first antimiscegenation law, preventing Englishwomen from marrying Negroes.

1688 In their monthly meeting the Pennsylvania Quakers raised the first formal protest against slavery in the colonies.

THE EIGHTEENTH CENTURY

1700 The number of enslaved people in the American colonies was approximately 28,000, the majority of whom (23,000) lived in the South. Samuel Sewall, a Boston merchant, and the Boston Committee of Massachusetts formally opposed the slave trade.

1708 By this time the enslaved population of the Carolinas outnumbered the European colonists there.

1731 African American Benjamin Banneker was born free in Maryland and was reared with his sisters on his father's tobacco farm. He was a self-taught astronomer and achieved fame as a scientist and inventor. Banneker is credited with assisting in laying out the city of Wash-

ington, DC. George Washington commissioned French engineer Pierre L'Enfant to survey and design the nation's capital, assisted by Andrew Ellicott and his assistant, Benjamin Banneker. The district's boundaries were laid out based on Ellicott and Banneker's mathematical and astronomical calculations. After many disputes arose among L'Enfant and district commissioners overseeing the city's development, L'Enfant was fired, leaving his plans incomplete. Ellicott and Banneker reproduced the plans from notes and memory, and the project continued without incident.

1738 Some Africans escaped from slavery in the North American colonies and founded their own settlement. The settlement was later disbanded in 1763 when the Spanish ceded Florida to Britain.

Our Developing Methodist Roots

In 1703 John Wesley was born in Epworth, England. In 1728, at the age of 25, he was ordained as a priest in the Church of England. John and his brother Charles Wesley were interested in a religion that included not only Bible study and prayer but a social consciousness that led them to take their message into the prisons and to preach in the streets and fields to the poor. When it became clear that John Wesley was no longer welcome to preach inside the Church of England, a new movement began to develop outside the church. Although John Wesley never officially left the Church of England, the Methodist Movement developed under his leadership. When the Methodist Movement eventually made its way to America, African Americans were part of the movement from its beginning.

In the remainder of the book, the chronology is divided into two columns that juxtapose events occurring in the world (first column) and events occurring in the The United Methodist Church (second column).

THE EIGHTEENTH CENTURY

1735 John and Charles Wesley came to America as missionaries in the colony of Georgia.

1743 John Wesley believed that slavery was a great evil and that Christians must reject and fight the evil. Wesley wrote into the General Rules the prohibition of "the buying or selling of the bodies and souls of men, women, and children, with an intention to enslave them."

1744 The first Methodist Conference was held in London. At this first conference were six clergymen of the Church of England and four lay preachers. This first session was spent in defining terms such as *repentance, saving faith, justification, sanctification, free will, the witness of the Spirit,* and other doctrines.

1746 Lucy Terry penned the first known English writing by an African American, "Bars Fight," a ballad about the conflict between Massachusetts colonists and Native Americans at The Bars, a meadow area outside Deerfield. The poem was not published until 1855.

1752 Benjamin Banneker, a self-taught African American scientist, constructed the first striking clock made entirely in America, from pieces he carved from wood.

1758 John Wesley baptized two Blacks into Methodism, at least one of whom was a woman.

The World

1770 Crispus Attucks, a black sailor, was the first to challenge the British troops, becoming the first to die in the Boston Massacre, the onset of the American Revolution. Many Blacks served in integrated units during the Revolutionary war.

Quakers opened a school for African Americans in Philadelphia.

1772 Britain's highest court ruled that slavery in the United Kingdom was unconstitutional.

1773 Phillis Wheatley published a book of poems, the first book published in America by an African American. She also

The United Methodist Church

1760 Richard Allen was born into slavery on February 14. He was converted to Christianity around age 17. Allen and his brother purchased their freedom around 1783.

1764 Anne Sweitzer, a slave known as Aunt Annie, was a founding member of the first Methodist society in America, located in Frederick County, Maryland.

Blacks were also members of Saint George's Methodist Episcopal Church in Philadelphia.

1771 Francis Asbury came to America to strengthen Methodist societies. Asbury was in favor of emancipation and led the Methodist movement against slavery. Asbury was active in the lives of the Methodist flock, preaching in all-Negro crowds, mixed crowds, and all-white crowds. His work among the societies helped the Methodist movement in America develop a mindset that, in general, disapproved of slavery.

wrote a poem in honor of General George Washington, to which Washington responded by inviting her for a visit.

The first black Baptist church under black leadership was founded in Silver Bluff, South Carolina, by George Liele, who was then a slave of Baptist deacon Henry Sharp.

1774 George Liele began preaching to Blacks in British-occupied Savannah, Georgia. Liele was later freed by his owner, Henry Sharp. He moved to Jamaica and founded the first black Baptist church there and a free school.

1775 Quakers in Pennsylvania organized the first abolition society in the United States, the Pennsylvania Society for the Abolition of Slavery.

The role of African Americans in the American Revolution, and the contribution they made in the cause of freedom for the new nation, are not often found in history books. But why wouldn't they be drawn to a war

1774 John Wesley wrote "Thoughts Upon Slavery." Among some of the thoughts he penned were: "I absolutely deny all slave-holding to be consistent with any degree of natural justice, mercy, and truth," and, "Liberty is the right of every human creature as soon as he breathes the vital air, and no human being can deprive him of that right which he derives from the law of nature." Although Wesley offered no plan of how to eliminate slavery, he remained steadfast against it. He appealed to the consciousness of Christianity as foundational for acceptance of all people as equals. Yet there were signs that the Methodist Movement was retreating on the slavery issue. The rule against traveling preachers owning slaves was cancelled for four states in the South.

for freedom? Perhaps as they fought valiantly at the battles of Lexington and Concord, they envisioned a better life for themselves and so many of their enslaved brothers.

- June 17: At the Battle of Bunker Hill, two African Americans distinguished themselves. They were Peter Salem and Salem Poor.
- July: An order by General George Washington's Adjutant General was issued to ban Negroes from the American Army.
- Early October: The council of general officers met to bar slaves and free African Americans from fighting in the war.
- October 23: The Continental Congress approved the resolution from the army.
- November 7: By then, the British were offering freedom to male slaves who would join their army.
- November 12: General George Washington, later to be known as "the father of his country," issued a general order forbidding recruiting officers to enlist African Americans.
- December 31: By then, situations had changed. General Washington reversed himself and ordered recruitment officers to accept free African American men.

1776 On July 4, the Second Continental Congress adopted the Declaration of Independence, ending ties between the American colonies and Great Britain.

1776 Most Methodist preachers from England, except for Asbury, left for home.

The World

Thomas Jefferson authored a passage in the document condemning slavery, but the passage was eliminated under pressure from Georgia and South Carolina delegates.

1777 Vermont was the first state to formally ban slavery within its borders, July 2.

Enslaved Africans in Massachusetts filed a legislative petition arguing that slavery was in conflict with the principles of the American Revolution. During the period of the war, eight such petitions were filed.

Over the next two and a half decades, seven more states (Pennsylvania, Massachusetts, New Hampshire, Connecticut, Rhode Island, New York, and New Jersey) enacted legislation or constitutional amendments supporting emancipation.

1778 Virginia formally abolished the slave trade. Slavery itself was not outlawed.

1778-1781 It is estimated that five thousand African Americans served as soldiers in the patriot armies during the American Revolution.

1779 Jean Baptiste Pointe duSable founded a riverside trading post. It would later become Chicago, Illinois.

The United Methodist Church

A black servant named Betty became a charter member of the John Street Methodist Society in New York City.

The World

1780 While the Christian church was not taking bold steps against slavery, some progress was being made in the country:

- Pennsylvania adopted a policy of gradual emancipation for enslaved Blacks.
- The first slave in the American colonies to be granted her freedom was Elizabeth Freeman in Great Barrington, Massachusetts.
- George Derham became the first African American licensed to practice medicine in the United States.
- Lemuel Haynes pastored an all-white congregation in Torrington, Connecticut, becoming the first African American to do so. Haynes was a former minuteman who had fought at the Battle of Lexington.

The global slave trade was at its height.

1781 Forty-four settlers founded the city of Los Angeles. Twenty-six of them were black.

1784 Phillis Wheatley, and African American poet, died on December 5 in Boston.

The United Methodist Church

1780 The first Methodist Conference in the United States was convened. One of the major issues was that of slavery. Although Methodists, particularly traveling preachers, were forbidden to own slaves, both clergy and bishops owned slaves.

According to the Minutes of the 1780 Methodist Annual Conference, the Conference framed, discussed, and approved the following questions:

> "Ought not this Conference to require those traveling preachers who hold slaves to give promise to set them free? Yes."

> "Does the Conference acknowledge that slavery is contrary to the laws of God, man, and nature, and hurtful to society; contrary to the dictates of conscience and pure religion, and doing that which we would not that others should do to us or ours? Do we pass our disapprobation on all our friends who keep slaves and advise their freedom? Yes."

This Conference also approved a statement providing for religious instruction for slaves and continuous exertion of pressure for emancipation. This legislation was later cancelled for four southern states. These were the first of years of appeasement for the South given by the church.

1784 The Christmas Conference marked the official organization of The Methodist Episcopal Church. It was held at

Lovely Lane Church in Baltimore, Maryland. The African Americans who were in attendance were Harry Hosier and Richard Allen. Harry had been one of the circuit riders to go out and spread the news about the conference and urge preachers to attend. During the conference Richard Allen was licensed to preach.

There were approximately 15,000 members in Methodist societies. Of these, only approximately 2,500 lived north of Maryland. (Various sources list conflicting counts, leaving one to conclude that some sources counted clergy only for certain purposes.)

1785 The Abolition Society in New York was organized.

1786 The first Sunday school was established by Francis Asbury. In 1790 the Methodist Conference established Sunday schools for both black and white children.

John Stewart was born of free parents in Virginia. John was converted to Christianity in 1816 and went on to become recognized for his missions work among the Wyandot Indians. (See 1816.)

1787 Prince Hall, a free Black of Boston, founded the first lodge in the Negro Masonic Order, now known as the Prince Hall Grand Lodge. Because of the state of race relations in America, the charter for the lodge was obtained in England.

1787 Richard Allen and Absalom Jones organized the Free African Society, the first Negro self-improvement institution for Blacks.

The World

Delegates in Philadelphia approved the new U.S. Constitution, which contained clauses protecting the institution of slavery.

A colony for freed slaves was established in Sierra Leone, Africa. It began with 377 settlers.

Prince Hall led Blacks from Boston in petitioning the legislature for equal school facilities.

The African Free School opened in New York.

1788
The U.S. Constitution was ratified. It contained the following provisions:

- It forbade Congress from prohibiting the importation of slaves for the next twenty years;
- It mandated that a "person held to service or labor" in one state be "delivered up on claim of the party to whom such service or labor shall be due."

A major issue arose about how to count the slave population, since population numbers affected taxes and representation in Congress. In some southern states the slave population outnumbered that of Whites. The

The United Methodist Church

African American worshippers, including Richard Allen, were pulled from a kneeling position while at prayer in St. George's Methodist Episcopal Church in Philadelphia. Allen and others had been accustomed to sitting around the edges of the sanctuary, but on this particular Sunday a sexton wanted them to go into the balcony. When the Blacks were seated and kneeling in prayer, the sexton and reinforcements pulled them to their feet. It was a most humiliating moment for the individuals but also a blight on the character of The Methodist Episcopal Church.

Some Blacks continued to worship at St. George's. Richard Allen and several African Americans began to worship apart from the organized Methodist Episcopal Church. Other Blacks began to worship on their own but did not join Allen.

Constitution enacted a compromise that further solidified the dehumanization of Blacks by counting them as three fifths of a person.

1789 The Enlightenment movement, based on rationality, progressive humanitarianism, and the logic of science, embraced the idea that all of humanity shared the birthright of freedom. The movement bolstered condemnation of the slave trade.

On August 26 the National Assembly of the revolutionary French government declared that "Men are born and remain free and equal in rights."

Olaudah Equiano, a slave who eventually returned to Africa, published his autobiography detailing his experiences under slavery.

1790 The first U.S. Census stated the black population to be 757,208. This was 19.3 percent of the total population. Of the black population, 59,557 were free. Slavery had been abolished in all the northern colonies.

1791 The United States Bill of Rights, the first ten amendments to the Constitution, was ratified.

Benjamin Banneker created his first of several annual almanacs. He sent one to Thomas Jefferson, who was secretary of state, protesting slavery and hoping to persuade Jefferson that Blacks were not intellectually inferior to Whites. Jefferson acknowledged the almanac and asked for further

1791 John Wesley wrote a letter denouncing slavery. In it, he wrote: "Go on, in the name of God and in the power of his might, till every American slavery (the vilest that ever saw the sun) shall vanish away before it."

proof "that nature has given to our [black] brethren talents equal to that of other colors of men." Jefferson later sent a copy to the Academy of Sciences in Paris.

1792 Benjamin Banneker published his first almanac, which calculated astronomical occurrences with remarkable accuracy.

Twelve hundred African Americans who lived in Nova Scotia resettled in Sierra Leone.

1793 With the invention of the cotton gin, the Southern cotton industry grew, and with it grew the demand for slave labor. Eli Whitney was issued a patent for the device on March 14, 1794.

With pressure by southern delegates, the U.S. Congress enacted the first fugitive slave law, which made it illegal to harbor an escaped slave. This made it difficult to provide assistance to escaping slaves.

1794 Congress outlawed the exportation of slaves from the United States to any other country.

1794 Richard Allen founded Bethel African Methodist Episcopal Church in Philadelphia, the first African American church in the North.

Zoar Church, the oldest continuous church, was founded in Philadelphia by African Americans who left St. George's Methodist Episcopal Church but did not follow Richard Allen. It is now known as Mother African Zoar United Methodist Church.

The World

1796 The Boston African Society was established by a group of African Americans. This was a mutual aid organization, one of several organizations developed to help African Americans help one another and those even less fortunate.

Joshua Johnson opened an art studio in Baltimore. Johnson was the first widely recognized African American painter.

The United Methodist Church

Other Blacks withdrew to follow Absalom Jones to The Episcopal Church, another predominantly white denomination. Jones and his followers dedicated the African Episcopal Church of St. Thomas in Philadelphia.

1796 Approximately thirty African Americans led by James Varick, Peter Williams, William Miller, Francis Jacobs, and others left John Street Methodist Episcopal Church in New York to hold separate worship services for Blacks. Since the church had several black preachers but no ordained black minister, they had to rely on white ministers to preach and supply Communion services. In 1800 the growing congregation built a house of worship that they named African Methodist Episcopal Zion Church, the first African American church in New York.

1797 Isabella Bomefree (Baumfree) was born in Ulster County, New York, to James and Elizabeth Bomefree, slaves to the prominent Dutch family of Johannes Hardenbergh. Isabella grew up speaking Dutch. New York had few slaves, and the land was not conducive to plantation-type agriculture. The worry of most slave families was that their children would be sold to strangers, particularly to be taken "down south." Isabella's mother, Ma Bet, instilled in her daughter the belief that she should always trust in God, pray, and listen for God's guidance. Isabella grew in her Christian spirituality. When she was thirty years old, after some haggling over her earned freedom, Isabella moved with one or two of her children to New York City. (See 1828.)

1799 Richard Allen was ordained.

THE NINETEENTH CENTURY

1800 At the end of the Eighteenth Century, seven of the original colonies were, at least technically, free states. The slave-holding states among the original colonies were Delaware, Georgia, Maryland, North Carolina, South Carolina, and Virginia. Other states who had joined the Union were Vermont, a free state, and Kentucky and Tennessee, slave states. As states were added to the Union, the balance was maintained between slave states and free states. Ohio, Illinois, and Indiana were admitted as free states, while Louisiana, Mississippi, and Alabama came in as slave states.

The population in the United States was over five million, and the African American population was over one million, 18.9 percent of the total.

Abolitionist John Brown was born in Connecticut.

John Brown

1800 The General Conference authorized the ordination of Blacks as deacons but did not permit the authorization to be printed as a rule in *The Book of Discipline*. The document titled "Regulation Respecting the Ordination of Colored People to the Office of Deacon" did not give Blacks full access to ministry and leadership in the church.

Our Developing Methodist Roots

Enslaved blacksmith Gabriel and his followers were stopped from a planned uprising against slavery in Richmond, Virginia, by a rainstorm. Betrayed by two other slaves, Gabriel and at least twenty-five of his followers were hanged. This was the first major slave rebellion planned in the United States.

1803 Denmark explicitly forbade trade in African slaves.

The ports of South Carolina were reopened to the slave trade from Latin America to satisfy the demand for labor in the newly acquired Louisiana Purchase.

Migration of escaped slaves and Native American Indian tribes to "Indian Territory" (now Oklahoma) began, followed in the 1820's and 1830's by mass migration of Native Americans forced by the U.S. Government and known as The Trail of Tears.

1804 The first of a series of Black Laws was enacted by the Ohio legislature. These laws restricted the movement of African Americans in the North. Other northern states followed suit in the years to come. Illinois, Indiana, and Oregon included anti-immigration clauses in their state constitutions.

1807 The British parliament banned the British colonies from taking part in the slave trade and from using British ships in such trade.

The World

1808 The U.S. Congress officially banned the importation of slaves. Illegal importation of slaves continued. (This was the first time such a ban was possible following a clause in the constitution of 1788 that prohibited such a ban for twenty years.)

All northern states had banned slavery by law, or had a law or constitutional provision that could be interpreted as doing so. No state in the South had done so. Slavery continued in both the North and the South.

1809 On February 12, Abraham Lincoln was born in Kentucky.

1812 African Americans distinguished themselves as sailors and militia for both armies in the War of 1812.

1815 Paul Cuffe, a prominent free person who was a ship owner and an early advocate of repatriation, made two trips to Africa in preparation for the resettlement of free and enslaved Blacks. He transported thirty-eight free Blacks to Sierra Leone. The idea of colonization was a debated issue. Cuffe and some others believed that Blacks would never be treated justly in the United States. Others, like Frederick Douglass, James Forten, and Richard Allen, fought for Blacks to remain in America and fight for justice.

The United Methodist Church

1808 Moral objection to slavery was deepening. Many voices in The Methodist Episcopal Church were being heard.

1812 Blacks were ordained as elders.

1816 There were approximately 42,200 black Methodists in The Methodist Episcopal Church.

The World

1817 The American Colonization Society was organized in the House of Representatives. The purpose was to encourage and support the transport of African Americans to Africa. While some Blacks supported such a movement because they felt they could not achieve racial equality in America, most Blacks opposed colonization.

1820 Eighty-six Blacks sailed on the Mayflower of Liberia to resettle in Liberia, on the west coast of Africa. This was a part of the American Colonization Society's efforts to move liberated slaves out of America.

The Missouri Compromise went into effect. This political arrangement stated that slavery was formally forbidden in a region of the Louisiana Territory north of the latitudinal line at 36 degrees 30 minutes. The

The United Methodist Church

Richard Allen formed the African Methodist Episcopal Church (AME) in Philadelphia. One thousand sixty-six black Methodists who withdrew from Methodist Episcopal Church congregations in Baltimore and Attleborough, Pennsylvania, became part of the new denomination. Allen was committed to Methodist doctrine and teachings and adopted most of the same policies. He was elected bishop of the new denomination on April 11, 1816.

John Stewart arrived in Upper Sandusky, Ohio, where he became an effective missionary among the Wyandot Indians. His ministry among the Wyandots led to Native Americans becoming a part of Methodism.

The World

Compromise was made when Maine, a free state, entered the Union at the same time the slave state of Missouri was admitted.

The British Navy stepped up efforts to suppress the slave trade.

1821 Thomas L. Jennings became the first African American to obtain a patent. The patent was for a dry-cleaning process.

New York City became the site of the first black acting troupe, the African Grove Theatre.

1822 Denmark Vesey, a respected free Black, organized an insurrection against the city of Charleston, South Carolina, in order to free the slaves. After he was betrayed, he and dozens of co-conspirators were executed following a long trial.

Hiram Revels, the first African American United States senator, was born free in Fayetteville, North Carolina.

1823 The first African American college graduate was Alexander Lucius Twilight, who earned a B.A. degree from Middlebury College in Vermont.

The African Grove Theatre produced the first play written and performed by an African American, Henry Brown's *Drama of King Shotaway*.

The United Methodist Church

1821 After trustees of the African Methodist Episcopal Zion Church agreed to no longer accept white control, James Varick and others led the church in reorganizing their denomination, The African Methodist Episcopal Zion Church (AMEZ). James Varick, who was ordained as an elder in 1820, was finally consecrated by Whites as the denomination's first bishop in 1822.

1824 The General Conference of The Methodist Episcopal Church authorized African American preachers to travel and preach where their services were necessary.

The World

1827 Ten thousand people were liberated when slavery was abolished in New York.

The first newspaper to be wholly owned and produced by African Americans, *Freedom's Journal*, was published in New York. John B. Russwurm and Samuel Cornish were the paper's founders. Russwurm has been identified as one of the first black graduates of a college in the United States. He graduated from Bowdoin College in 1826. Russwurm later abandoned journalism and became an advocate for colonization.

The United Methodist Church

Isabella Bomefree

1828 Isabella Bomefree (Baumfree) joined The Methodist Episcopal Church on John Street in New York. She became a part of an interracial reform movement in the city interested in starting a spiritual revival among the unchurched. She later became a member of The African Methodist Episcopal Zion Church, formed by some Blacks who were former members of John Street. Expanding her ministry beyond the congregation, Bomefree worked with a variety of groups as she continued to spread the Word. She eventually took the name Sojourner Truth, as she believed that God was calling her to wander from place to place spreading the Word. She later became a strong advocate for women's rights and spoke out against slavery. Though she never learned to read or write, she remembered portions of

Scripture and expounded from them. She often got children to read the Bible for her because she did not trust adults to read without their personal biases.

A number of people became disenchanted with The Methodist Episcopal Church. A major issue was that all the leadership of the church was clergy. In November a convention of these disenchanted churches met in Baltimore, Maryland, and formed The Associated Methodist Churches. Another convention was called in 1830—when a constitution was completed—and the name was changed to The Methodist Protestant Church. This split in the church was the first split that was not based on race.

1829
White mobs attacked African Americans in Cincinnati, Ohio, during a three-day race riot. Approximately one thousand, half of the city's black population, fled into Canada.

Sister Elizabeth Lange, a Haitian nun, established the first African American women's religious order in the United States. The Oblate Sisters of Providence was founded in Baltimore.

1830
The first National Negro Convention met in Philadelphia. Delegates met to discuss and agree on self-help measures. Richard Allen presided.

1831
William Lloyd Garrison, abolitionist, launched *The Liberator*, which quickly became the most influential newspaper of the antislavery movement. In 1832 Garrison led a group in forming the New England Anti-Slavery Society in Boston, a group dedicated to the immediate emancipation of slaves.

The World

The Southampton Massacre, in which approximately sixty white people were killed by slaves, occurred in Virginia. Nat Turner led the rebellion in August and was captured in October. He was hanged in November in Jerusalem, Virginia.

1833 Ira Aldridge debuted as the first black actor at Royal Coburg Theatre in London. He went on to star in about sixty roles, some of the most famous being Shakespearean characters. He performed in countries around the world and was showered with honors for his versatile and powerful acting abilities.

1834 Slavery was abolished in England and its empire, freeing over 700,000 people.

Henry Blair received a patent for his corn-planting machine

1835 The American Anti-Slavery Society was operating at full force. It produced numerous publications that reached hundreds of thousands of people, employed lecturing agents, conducted an extensive petition drive, and organized hundreds of auxiliary societies. The Society raised huge sums of money and expended it toward the cause.

The United Methodist Church

1832 The General Conference of The Methodist Episcopal Church approved that power be given to bishops to appoint African American preachers to the black congregations, but these African American preachers were not yet full members of annual conferences.

1835 Throughout Methodism, African Americans continued to worship with Whites even though they had to occupy separate seating designated for them by the Whites. In Baltimore, Maryland, ten black congregations of Methodists were in existence.

The World

In New York City, African Americans formed a committee to help fugitive slaves escape to freedom.

1836 Congress adopted a gag rule prohibiting debate on any antislavery legislation. This rule remained in effect until 1844.

Alexander Lucius Twilight was elected to a seat in the Vermont legislature, making him the first African American elected to public office.

1837 The first Anti-Slavery Convention of American Women was held in New York City. Ten percent of the participants were black women.

1839 On August 24 the *Amistad* slave ship landed off Long Island, New York, thrusting the Supreme Court of the United States into the position of determining whether the Africans would be set free or sent into slavery. The Court ruled that the Africans, defended by former president John Adams, had never been slaves and their capture had violated an agreement of international law. The thirty-five survivors of the original fifty-three were set free in 1841 and returned to the shores of Africa in January 1842.

The United Methodist Church

The Methodist Episcopal Church opposed the work of the antislavery societies. The church began to bring to trial those ministers who identified themselves as abolitionists or promoted antislavery ideas. The following conferences took such action: Ohio in 1835; Baltimore and New York in 1836; Philadelphia, Pittsburg, and Michigan in 1838. The fact that these were not southern states lends credibility to the view that the majority church in the North was yielding to the pressures of the South.

The World

The Liberty Party, an antislavery political party, was first organized in Warsaw, New York. The party became official the following year.

1840 The African American population was over 2.8 million.

1841 Frederick Douglass made his first antislavery speech in Nantucket, Massachusetts.

The United Methodist Church

1840 The number of African Americans in The Methodist Episcopal Church reached 87,197. This number was due in part to the number of "plantation missions." In spite of the discriminatory policies and practices of the church, many Blacks remained because of the strong stances against slavery by Asbury, Coke, and other Methodist leaders.

Friction was growing between the abolitionists and the leaders in The Methodist Episcopal Church. At the General Conference, the bishops sought to keep the issue of slavery at bay by espousing that they did not believe that additional action would be helpful. However, the bishops had clearly misread the sentiment of the members, because there were no fewer than fifty-five petitions and memorials on the question of slavery. There was a Committee on Slavery of the General Conference. The Committee really did not wish to act on these petitions and came back with a report requesting to be discharged from their tasks. A motion was made to recommit to the committee's work. The stage was set for a showdown on the slavery issue, one the general church had tried to avoid.

The World

1843 The Liberty Party met in Buffalo. For the first time, African Americans participated in a national political gathering. Samuel R. Ward led the convention in prayer. Charles B. Ray was a convention secretary, and Henry Highland Garnet was a member of the nominating committee.

Norbert Rillieux, the son of a French planter father and a slave mother, was granted a patent for an evaporator device that revolutionized the sugar industry.

The United Methodist Church

1842 Orange Scott, LeRoy Sunderland, and other staunch abolitionists led a small group of preachers and laypeople out of The Methodist Episcopal Church. In 1843 they formed The Wesleyan Connection, later known as The Wesleyan Church. They wanted the church to resolve the issue of slavery once and for all. Their stance was a strong moral challenge over the issue of slavery.

1843 Sojourner Truth (Isabella Bomefree) began her abolitionist work.

1844 Since 1784 there had been sharp conflicts within the church over the issue of slavery. Sixty years of struggling with "what to do about the Negroes" finally resulted in a dramatic split. Precipitating the crisis of separation was an issue regarding Bishop James O. Andrew and his ownership of a slave. Apparently sometime between 1840 and 1844 the bishop had been bequeathed a young slave girl, Kitty. She was to be held until she was old enough to be sent to Liberia. The story is told that she refused to go; however, that is unlikely given the times, since the young woman would not have been able to make decisions of her own free will. Nevertheless, the laws of Georgia prohibited the bishop from freeing her. The bishop also received a male slave, and the story was again that the male refused to go North to be free.

The issue came to the 1844 General Conference. A resolution known as the Finley resolution called for the bishop to desist from carrying out the responsibilities of the office of bishop until he had freed himself from being a slave owner. The resolution passed on June 1, 1844, with a vote of 110 in favor and 68 against. This action precipitated the grand split of the church, and a plan of separation proposed by fifty-two southern delegates was adopted.

The church now had three distinct divisions. The northern group retained the name Methodist Episcopal Church. The southern group took the name Methodist Episcopal Church, South. The Methodist Protestant Church, which had split off earlier, also remained in existence.

While the major issue no doubt centered on slavery, another issue was the understanding of the episcopacy. The northern church viewed bishops as accountable to the General Conference. The southern church accepted the election of bishops by the General Conference but felt that bishops were responsible or accountable to the areas in which they served.

The Methodist Episcopal Church did not abandon its interest in slaves, but hostilities made it difficult to carry out work with the slaves. The separate Negro churches of the northern branch of

The World

1845 Frederick Douglass lectured in Britain on the abolition of slavery and published one of his autobiographies, *Narrative of the Life of Frederick Douglass.*

Macon B. Allen became the first African American admitted to the bar and began his practice of law in Massachusetts.

1847 Frederick Douglass began publishing *The North Star.*

David J. Peck became the first African American to graduate from a United States medical school.

1849 Mammy Pleasant arrived in San Francisco and helped shape the city over the years to come.

Harriet Tubman escaped from slavery and began conducting the Underground Railroad, bringing out hundreds of slaves, including her parents.

Benjamin Roberts became the first to file an integration lawsuit when his daughter was denied admission to the Boston public school system. He lost the decision.

The United Methodist Church

Methodism were included in the white conferences. Having grown accustomed to their separate worshiping congregations, Negroes repeatedly requested to form their own conferences. This request was always denied.

1845 The organizing conference of delegates for the Methodist Episcopal Church, South was convened.

1846 The first General Conference of the Methodist Episcopal Church, South met in Petersburg, Virginia.

Among the number of African Americans traveling west to California to prospect for gold was Waller Jackson.

1850

There were 434,495 free Blacks and 3,204,313 slaves living in the United States. The total number of free and enslaved Blacks reflected about 15.7 percent of the total population.

Estimates suggest that by 1850, 36 million Africans had been sold into captivity or had died as a result of the slave trade.

Congress passed the Compromise of 1850, admitting California into the Union as a free state and decreeing that the status of Utah and New Mexico would be determined by the local residents. The fugitive slave laws were rewritten to appease southerners, giving broader options for slave catchers and penalties for those aiding runaway slaves. This compromise was an attempt to maintain national unity and to create balance between the powerful political interests of the South and the North, where the abolitionist movement was growing. Perhaps it did not register that the entire social, cultural, and economic system of the South revolved around the institution of slavery. The Compromise also outlawed slavery in the District of Columbia. It would take a few more years, however, for slavery to be eliminated.

The first African American woman to earn a bachelor of literature degree from a four-year college was Lucy Stanton, who graduated from Oberlin college in Ohio.

The World

1851 William C. Nell, abolitionist, published the first extensive history of the American Negro, *Services of Colored Americans in the Wars of 1776 and 1812.*

1852 The first edition of *Uncle Tom's Cabin* was published.

1854 The Kansas-Nebraska Act was passed, repealing the Missouri Compromise and opening Northern territory to slavery.

The first Negro college, Ashmum Institute, was founded in Chester County, Pennsylvania. It later became Lincoln University.

1857 The Supreme Court's decision in the Dred Scott case struck a blow against freedom. Dred Scott had been taken by his master into Illinois, a free state, to live for a number of years. Later he was taken back into Missouri, a slave state. Scott petitioned the court, claiming that he had a right to freedom because he had lived in a free state for a

The United Methodist Church

1856 Members of The Methodist Episcopal Church and the African Methodist Episcopal Church (AME) united in establishing Wilberforce University for Blacks. This action was a result of a committee appointed in 1853 by the Cincinnati Conference of the Methodist Episcopal Church. In 1862 Wilberforce University became the first African American university under the administration of African Americans. The school was sold to the AME Church for ten thousand dollars in 1863.

1857 Black and white Methodist missionaries preached to mixed audiences in South Carolina.

number of years. Eventually the case went to the Supreme Court, which ruled that Scott was not a citizen and was not entitled to bring a lawsuit. The court went on to say that the ban on slavery was unconstitutional and that no free Black could claim to be a citizen of the United States. The South was jubilant at the ruling, but there were angry protests in the North. The abolitionist movement won many supporters.

1858 William Wells Brown, believed to be the first African American playwright, published *The Escape*.

Abraham Lincoln was defeated in a campaign for the United States Senate. The famed Lincoln-Douglas debates gave Lincoln the opportunity to gain national recognition for his antislavery views.

Abraham Lincoln

1859 In possibly the largest slave auction in history, 436 people were sold in Savannah, Georgia, in an event so large that it was held at a racetrack. During such auctions, known as "weeping times," family ties were ignored and families torn apart, with some exceptions for mothers with young children and some husbands and wives.

White abolitionist John Brown and a small group including African Americans attempted to raid a federal arsenal at Harper's Ferry, Virginia. Their intent was to arm slaves for a rebellion. Brown and two of his followers were caught and hanged.

1858 The northern Methodist Episcopal Church elected Francis Burns as the first black bishop. Since the prevailing view was that Blacks could not oversee Whites, he was deployed to Liberia.

The World

1860 Abraham Lincoln was elected to the presidency on November 6. His platform included opposition to the admission of new states if they permitted slavery, thus his election prompted a secessionist movement. South Carolina seceded first, in December, and other states soon followed. Eleven states seceded and named themselves the Confederate States of America.

1861 The increased strength of the abolition movement, abolishment of slavery by northern states, and growing questions regarding the immoral implications of slavery splintered the country along North-South lines. On April 12, Fort Sumter was fired upon by Confederate soldiers and the Civil War, also known as the War Between the States, was on. The Confederate military was first to conscript African Americans for service, not for fighting but for the manual labor needed to free Whites for fighting. For almost two years African Americans tried to enlist in the Union army to fight for their own freedom. At first rebuffed, they were finally allowed to enlist when the Secretary of the Navy authorized enlistment of Negro slaves. There were approximately 160 all-black units. Negro soldiers participated in over 200 battles.

1862 An act of Congress abolished slavery in Washington, DC.

Congress forbade Union officers to capture and return slaves.

The United Methodist Church

1861 There were over 200,000 Blacks in the Methodist Episcopal Church at the onset of the Civil War. Following the war, the number would be greatly reduced to approximately 78,000. Upon obtaining their freedom, many former slaves left for new places and new expressions of faith. Some Blacks were chided and intimidated by family and friends who had become a part of the new all-black denominations; but some stayed, refusing to leave a denomination they had helped start!

1863

On January 1 President Abraham Lincoln signed the Emancipation Proclamation and the slaves were freed, yet it would take more than the stroke of a pen to make freedom a reality. Two more years of war ensued.

Two all-black units defeated Confederate forces at Milliken's Bend.

One of the bloodiest race riots occurred in New York. Fear of Blacks and hostility about their enlistment in the Union army sent mobs of Whites on a rampage. Blacks were murdered and hung on lampposts.

While many African American men proved themselves as outstanding fighters, one female war hero was Harriet Tubman. Tubman led an attack on rice fields in South Carolina, destroying food and goods important to the Confederate forces. She led hundreds of slaves to freedom as a conductor on the Underground Railroad and served as a nurse, cook, and spy for the Union army.

Led by a white officer from Boston, the Massachusetts 54th Regiment was made up of African American troops primarily from Massachusetts and Pennsylvania but also from over twenty northern and southern states. In a vain attack on Fort Wagner, the troops fought valiantly, and war heroes were made. The battle would later be depicted in the movie *Glory,* starring African American actor Denzel Washington.

The World

1864 Congress repealed the Fugitive Slave Laws and granted black Union troops equal pay with white troops.

1865 General Lee's surrender at Appomattox on April 9 ended the war.

On April 14, President Lincoln was shot by an assassin. He died the next day.

The thirteenth amendment was passed. The amendment outlawed slavery in the United States.

White legislatures in former rebel states enacted Black Codes that restricted the rights and freedom of movement of freed Blacks.

Congress approved the establishment of the National Freedmen's Bureau.

The United Methodist Church

1864 After forty years of petitioning, the first black conferences were organized in The Methodist Episcopal Church. The Delaware Mission Conference was organized in Philadelphia at the John Wesley Church, now Tindley Temple, on July 19. The Washington Mission Conference was organized in Baltimore, Maryland, on October 27. The General Conference adopted the black conferences as mission conferences.

The Methodist Episcopal Church numbered 984,933. This number included 28,634 black members.

A major question continued for the church: What about the "colored" people?

1865 On Thursday, January 12, twenty black religious leaders were invited to meet with Major-General William Sherman at one of the stateliest and most elegant southern mansions, where he had headquartered after his conquest of Savannah. Among the preachers in that meeting was William Bentley, 72, pastor of Andrews Chapel Meth-odist Episcopal Church, the only one of the denomination in Savannah. Rev. Bentley had been a slave until he was twenty-five years old. He had been in the ministry for twenty years. His congregation numbered 360 and had church property valued at $20,000.

The Mississippi Mission Conference organized in New Orleans on December 25. The reality of what it meant to have four million

1866 On January 9 Fisk University, a historically black institution, opened in Nashville, Tennessee.

The Civil Rights Act was enacted, giving all African Americans full citizenship. The bill was passed over the President's veto.

The emergence of the Ku Klux Klan and other terrorist groups initiated a reign of terror against free Blacks in the south. Pulaski, Tennessee, was the birthplace of the Klan.

In Memphis, Tennessee, a violent rampage led to the deaths of forty-six African Americans. Ninety homes, twelve schools, and four churches were burned.

The first two African Americans elected to an American legislative assembly were Edward G. Walker and Charles L. Mitchell, both of whom were elected to the Massachusetts House of Representatives.

African Americans set free without even the rudiments of basic skills was apparent in this organizing conference. For example, they could not write; therefore, when the presiding bishop called for the election of a secretary, they had to elect John P. Newman, a white minister.

Two years later in 1867 the Mississippi Mission Conference was divided into two conferences.

1866 John W. Roberts was the second black bishop elected. He served in Africa as a missionary bishop.

The South Carolina Mission Conference organized in Charleston, South Carolina, on April 2.

On August 7 a group of ministers and laymen met in a called meeting at Trinity Methodist Episcopal Church in Cincinnati, Ohio. They unanimously passed a resolution calling for the organization of a Freedmen's Aid Society of the Methodist Episcopal Church. One of their reports alluded to their mammoth task. How does an organization, no matter how well-intentioned, deal with millions of people who have no education, no skills, and no understanding of the social and political waters into which they have been thrust? While the pen had made them free, it would take much more than that to make them citizens. It is a testament to the moral effect of the church and to their own relationship with God that African American people were able to experience joy at legal freedom that spawned hope for education, for family, and for ability to move to and fro, and that they were able to establish themselves as persons of worth, no longer chattel.

Work was carried forth for several years before the articles of incorporation of the Freedmen's Aid Society were adopted. The Society, however, faced struggles brought about by the fact that the freedmen

- had suffered the psychological and social effects of slavery;
- were illiterate and believed by many to be inferior and unable to learn;
- were economically helpless;
- had been separated from the support of families;
- were untrained for work other than menial labor;
- were not citizens and had no rights;
- had no skills for living in freedom.

On October 11 the Tennessee Mission Conference organized in Murfreesboro. Later, the state was divided into two conferences. (See 1880.)

1867
The First Reconstruction Act was passed by Congress and included voting rights for all citizens.

1867
At Houston, Texas, the Texas Mission Conference was organized on January 3. It was divided into two conferences in 1874.

The Georgia Mission Conference was organized on October 10.

1868
Congress approved the fourteenth amendment, which granted full civil rights for African Americans.

1868
The North Carolina Mission Conference was organized on January 14.

Eight mission conferences began to function as annual conferences, but without voting rights or delegates to the General Conference. However, the mission conferences did send delegates. The General Conference debated for ten days and voted to rescind the rule against mission conference delegates. The General Conference then voted to give the status of annual conference to the mission conferences. They then seated two representatives as delegates.

The General Conference gave approval for the Freedmen's Aid Society but commended it to the annual conferences. This action in essence gave annual conferences the option to support it or not.

1869

Three more black conferences were organized. The Mississippi Conference was organized in Holly Springs on January 7. This conference was formed from a division of the originally organized conference. It would later form another conference called the Upper Mississippi Conference. (See 1891.)

New Orleans was the site of the organization of the Louisiana Conference on January 13.

The mostly white Kentucky Annual Conference met in annual session in Newport, Kentucky, and addressed a request from several black ministers in the conference to be formed into their own conference. The Kentucky Conference adopted a resolution and took it to the General Conference the same year, and it was approved. The new black conference was named Lexington Conference. Dr. Walter H. Riley said of the founding fathers in *Forty Years in the Lap of Methodism* (1915):

> The times of our fathers were times of persecution, but nothing hedged their way and kept them back from planting the banner of the gospel over every cabin.
>
> They were rough and illiterate, but they knew the way of salvation and did not hesitate to publish it while they tunneled the mountains, bridged the streams and felled trees in order that they might lay the foundation of the Lexington Conference.

Clark Seminary, the forerunner of Clark College, was established in Atlanta, Georgia.

1870

African Americans had begun to be involved in political activity in the South. Hiram Revels of Mississippi became the first African American elected to the United States Senate.

The thirteenth, fourteenth, and fifteenth amendments (ratified in 1865, 1868, and 1870 respectively) legally guaranteed freedom and citizenship, but complete and full citizenry rights were still a long way off.

1870

The Colored Methodist Episcopal Church (changed to Christian Methodist Episcopal in 1954) organized in 1870 after Blacks in The Methodist Episcopal Church, South petitioned the 1866 General Conference for their organization into separate congregations, districts, and annual conferences. Most of the African American members still remaining in The Methodist Episcopal Church, South went into the CME. In an effort to appease the white church, the articles of incorporation included statements disallowing political activity on church grounds.

1872

The first African American to serve as a state governor was Pinckney B. S. Pinchback, who was appointed interim governor in Louisiana.

1872

The General Conference placed the Freedmen's Aid Society in the benevolent associations of the general church.

For several decades the work of education for youth was carried out under the name and guidance of the society.

1873 The biracial Florida Conference formed in Jacksonville. Later an all-white conference was formed and the Florida Conference became all-black. The all-black conference became the South Florida Conference in 1925.

1874 The West Texas Conference was organized in Austin.

1876 The first request for a name change of the Freedmen's Aid Society came at this session of the General Conference. The first resolution was presented by R. W. Hammett from Arkansas. When it failed, another delegate offered a similar resolution, which was also rejected. Ironically, the Freedmen's Aid Society was assisting not only freed African Americans but also white children and youth, the South's economy having been devastated by the war.

The Central Alabama Conference was organized October 18 at Talladega. It was divided into two conferences in 1900, and then reunited in 1908.

The Savannah Conference was organized November 1. The Atlanta Conference evolved from this conference in 1896.

The World

The United Methodist Church

In October, Meharry Medical College, the first all-black medical school, was opened in Nashville, Tennessee, by the Freedmen's Aid Society. The first contributions to the school were made by Samuel Meharry and his four brothers. Their gifts were matched by the Methodist Episcopal Church. Meharry was organized as a department of Central Tennessee College, which was founded in the Clark Methodist Episcopal Church (later Clark Memorial United Methodist Church).

1877
Howard University was founded in Washington, DC, and Hampton Institute was founded in Hampton, Virginia.

1879
The Little Rock Conference was organized in Van Buren. It later became part of the new Southwest Conference.

1880
Continued efforts to change the name of the Freedmen's Aid Society and to place it under the supervision of the Board of Education of the church arose during this session of the General Conference. While rejecting the resolutions for name changes, the General Conference agreed to expand the work of the society among white populations.

The 1880 General Conference gave approval for work among Negro women and girls by the women of the church. The women wasted no time in going about their work. On June 8, 1880, in Trinity Methodist Episcopal Church in Cincinnati, Ohio, a new organization was formed. The Women's Home Missionary Society formed, with recommendation for special attention to the southern field. The first president was

Mrs. Rutherford B. Hayes, the First Lady of the land. Many of the women were wives of founders of the Freedmen's Aid Society.

The East Tennessee Conference formed in Greeneville as a result of the division of the Tennessee Conference.

1881 Frederick Douglass became recorder of deeds for Washington, DC.

The first Jim Crow law was enacted in Tennessee.

1883 Eatonville, Florida, became the first all-black incorporated town.

1881 At the meeting of the Lexington Conference in Springfield, Ohio, statistics listing the number of churches and membership were published for the first time. The minutes reflect that there were 105 churches with a membership of 7,189.

1884 The work of the Freedmen's Aid Society had expanded and was offering help to Whites as well as Blacks. Problems arose because of continued segregation and oppressive measures against African Americans in the South. The General Conference continued to maintain the name and policies of the Freedmen's Aid Society.

1887 The Central Missouri Conference organized in Sedalia. The Conference was terminated in 1928.

One of few known African American women serving the church through the Women's Home Missionary Society was Emma Virginia Levi (later Brown). She was from New Bedford, Massachusetts, and became a missionary and matron at Browning House in Camden, South Carolina, one of the society's industrial homes for girls. Other black women serving industrial homes included Mrs. Marcus Dale and Mrs. Hester Williams, an ex-slave, who worked ardently in homes in Louisiana, as did Mrs. Isabella Howells in Texas.

1888 The General Conference yielded to continued pressure from the South for a name change of the Freedmen's Aid Society. The name was changed to Freedmen's Aid and Southern Education Society. For twenty years this committee carried out educational work for Blacks and Whites.

1889 Rev. Charles N. Grandison became the first black president of Bennett College and the first black president of any of the institutions founded by the Freedmen's Aid Society. John P. Morris became the first black teacher in the subjects of Greek and Mathematics.

1891 The Upper Mississippi Conference was formed out of division of the Mississippi Conference. Both conferences existed through the 1939 unification.

1893 Dr. Daniel Hale Williams performed the first successful open-heart surgery in Chicago, Illinois, at Provident Hospital, which he had founded two years earlier.

THE TWENTIETH CENTURY

1900
The United States population stood at 75,991,575. The African American population was 8,833,994, or 11.6 percent of the country's occupants.

The number of African Americans working in professional jobs had grown to more than 47,000, including 21,267 teachers; 15,528 preachers; 2,000 actors and showmen; 1,734 doctors; 728 lawyers; 310 journalists; 247 photographers; 236 artists; 212 dentists; and one African American congressman. African Americans had also invested more than $500,000 in funeral homes.

A race riot in New Orleans in July resulted in the shooting of twenty-seven white people. An African American school and thirty African American homes were burned.

James Weldon Johnson and J. Rosamond Johnson, two brothers, composed the hymn "Lift Every Voice and Sing." Africa Americans have historically identified the song as the "the black national anthem." The third and last verse is a prayer and is usually sung more softly and reverently.

Booker T. Washington published *Up From Slavery*, an autobiography.

The National Negro Business League was organized in Boston, Massachusetts, in August.

1900
There were nineteen black conferences; 1,705 clergy; 3,398 churches; and 235,274 black Methodists.

The Lexington Conference branch of the Women's Home Missionary Society was organized on March 23, 1900, at Ninth Street Church in Covington, Kentucky. The following officers were elected: Mrs. J. T. Leggett, President; Mrs. Dollie Lewis, Vice President; Mrs. Emma Harris, Corresponding Secretary; Miss Ella B. Brown, Recording Secretary; Mrs. Corbin, Treasurer; Mrs. A. B. Vest, Mrs. M. E. Scarce, Mrs. Garner, and Mrs. D. E. Skelton, Managers.

The Mobile Conference was formed as a spin-off when the Central Alabama Conference was divided. The conferences were merged again in 1908 and named the Central Alabama Conference.

1902 The Oklahoma-Nebraska (Okaneb) Conference was organized and included all work with Blacks. The conference was dissolved in 1903.

1903 The Lincoln Conference replaced the Okaneb Conference.

1903 W.E.B. DuBois published *The Souls of Black Folk*, which crystallized DuBois's opposition to Booker T. Washington's position of political accommodation in favor of economic progress. The book became a classic, a must-read for African Americans.

Maggie Lena Walker, a shrewd businesswoman, established the St. Luke Penny Savings Bank.

The Supreme Court upheld the portion of the Alabama constitution that disenfranchised African Americans.

1904 Isaiah B. Scott from the Texas Conference was consecrated as bishop and then deployed to Liberia, where he served twelve years before retiring in 1916.

1905 The *Chicago Defender*, a black newspaper, began publication. It was a champion of African American rights. The uniqueness of this publication was that it was published for the masses, many of whom were illiterate. News focused on what was happening in their communities and churches.

1906 Paul Lawrence Dunbar, a distinguished poet, died in Dayton, Ohio.

After the Civil War, black soldiers continued to be viewed with contempt in southern states. In August, African American soldiers were accused of raiding Brownsville, Texas, although there was evidence that the soldiers could not have been involved. Soldiers were rounded up, and 167 were court-martialed without legal and fair hearings. They were dishonorably discharged by order of President Roosevelt, creating hardships for them in the areas of employment, pensions, and medical care. (The rulings were reversed in 1962.)

Martial law was declared in Atlanta, Georgia, after a race riot in September killed ten African Americans and two Whites.

1908 Thurgood Marshall was born in Baltimore, Maryland, on July 2.

In the Springfield, Illinois, riots, a mob of several thousand Whites attempted to abduct two African American men from a local jail. One of the men was innocent, having been falsely accused of raping a white woman who later admitted that she had lied. The men had been moved to a safer location, and when the mob discovered that there was no one to lynch, they moved on to a black neighborhood. The mob, fortified by an orgy of drinking, began burning, shooting, and looting in the community. Whites who had businesses or houses in the neighborhood put white handkerchiefs outside so that the rioters would know that the building

1907 The first African American staff person for the Women's Home Missionary Society was Miss Bessie Garrison, who became a field worker. Several other African Americans succeeded her in years to come.

1908 The General Conference met in Baltimore, Maryland. During this session, the work of the Board of Education was redistributed, assigning white schools of the South to the care of the Board of Education, creating a new board for the work of Sunday school interests, and restoring the Freedmen's Aid Society's original name. Twenty-two schools for Whites were taken out of the society's control. Educational work for Negroes of the Methodist Episcopal Church continued under the name of the Freedmen's Aid Society until May 1920. The General Conference thus continued appeasement of the South at the sacrifice of African Americans!

was owned by Whites. This riot was a turning point for many, both white and black, who began to express concern and to act on their concerns. These concerns were influential in the establishment of the National Association for the Advancement of Colored People (NAACP) the next year.

1909

The National Association for the Advancement of Colored People (NAACP), a new civil rights organization, was formed on February 12, the anniversary of Abraham Lincoln's hundredth birthday. NAACP founders included W.E.B. DuBois, Ida B. Wells-Barnett, and Mary Church Terrell. The purpose of the organization was to oppose racial segregation, promote racial equality, and seek justice. The first meeting was called in response to the Springfield race riots and drew only seven African Americans and more than fifty Whites.

Matthew Henson, a black man, was the first man to reach the North Pole, followed by Robert E. Peary, a white man, who was pulled on a sled by four Eskimos because his toes were frostbitten. Henson planted the flag at the spot where Peary said the North Pole was. Henson has since been recognized for his role during that expedition.

THE DECADE OF THE 1910'S

1910

The African American population reached 9,827,763, or 10.7 percent of the total population

The World

1911 The National Urban League (originally called the National League on Urban Conditions Among Negroes) was formed as an interracial social service organization with focus on resettlement assistance to those migrating north, education, vocational training, and other direct services. Later it added research and lobbying components to its services.

1912 Garrett A. Morgan invented the gas mask, which was originally used for firefighters. Morgan was also granted a patent for the traffic light. He was an African American and the son of former slaves.

1913 Harriet Tubman, who had helped several hundred people to freedom on the Underground Railroad, died in Auburn, New York, on March 10.

The United Methodist Church

1911 The Commission on Union, meeting January 18–20 in Cincinnati, Ohio, considered several papers proposing plans for reunion of the Methodist church bodies. Previous efforts to unite the church had been met with southern plans for a segregated church. As a matter of fact and of record, it seemed that few voices in the South considered anything less than a segregated church. This commission meeting was no exception. More than one paper presented to the commission suggested that the best solution would be to form one church that included all the African members of the Methodist Episcopal Church with the members of the Colored Methodist Episcopal Church, the African Methodist Episcopal Church, and the African Methodist Episcopal Church Zion.

The segregationist pattern of thinking was as consistent in the church as it was in American society and culture. Needless to say, there was no indication that those African Americans who had left, nor those who had stayed, desired an all-black and segregated church.

The World

1914 World War I began.

1915 The NAACP awarded the first Spingarm Medal to biologist Ernest E. Just. The award was created to honor outstanding African Americans. Ernest E. Just conducted pioneering research on fertilization, artificial parthenogenesis, and cell division.

The Ku Klux Klan received its charter from the Superior Court of Fulton County, Georgia. Klan chapters began to form in Alabama and other southern states.

The Great Migration reached its height. As many as 1.5 million African Americans moved from southern states to northern industrialized states.

The NAACP organized protest demonstrations against the showing of the movie *Birth of a Nation*.

On September 9 Dr. Carter G. Woodson, historian, founded the Association for the Study of Negro Life and History (ASNLH). This organization was formed partly in response to the film *Birth of a Nation* and also as an alternative to the American Historical Society, which ignored the existence and contributions of African Americans. The ASNLH used scholarship to refute erroneous and racist ideas about African Americans.

The United Methodist Church

1915 Rev. Robert E. Jones, editor of the *Southwestern Christian Advocate*, a strong black leader and an outspoken voice on racial matters (and a future bishop) made the following statement in a speech at Northwestern University: "If the church draws the color line, then the preachers of hate and segregation will have gained a forceful endorsement of their propaganda, which is as undemocratic, as un-American, as it is unChristian."

1916 Alexander P. Camphor from Central Alabama, who graduated from Gammon, was consecrated as a bishop.

1917
The United States entered World War I on April 6. Over 350,000 African American soldiers were involved in the conflict. Some thought that showing patriotism would lead to voting rights and equality of other rights. But African Americans served in segregated units because white soldiers did not want to fight alongside them. African American soldiers had to fight the enemy *and* American citizens. The NAACP fought for the establishment of a Colored Officers Training Camp, which was established in Iowa.

Martial law was declared after a race riot in East Saint Louis, Illinois, in which African American deaths were estimated at between forty and two hundred.

Approximately 10,000 African Americans marched silently down New York's Fifth Avenue to protest lynchings and other racial indignities.

A race riot broke out in Houston, Texas, between the all-black 24th Infantry Regiment and the white citizens. Four African Americans and sixteen Whites were killed. Martial law was declared. Nineteen members of the regiment were later court-martialed and hanged.

The Supreme Court struck down an ordinance in Louisville, Kentucky, that required Blacks and Whites to live in separate blocks.

1918
Race riots continued to punctuate the life of African Americans, not just in the South but in the North as well. In July

riots occurred in both Chester and Philadelphia in Pennsylvania.

World War I came to an end, and the armistice was signed November 11. African Americans had furnished approximately 370,000 soldiers and 1,400 commissioned offices. Three African American regiments received awards for valor. Several soldiers were decorated for bravery.

1919

Race riots broke out across the United States. Twenty-six riots and nearly eighty brutal lynchings occurred during what is known as "Red Summer." Several African American veterans were lynched in their uniforms. Riots took place in Texas, Tennessee, and Arkansas in the South, and in Washington, DC, Illinois, and Nebraska in the North. "Red Summer" marked the first time African Americans were willing to fight for their rights.

In Longview, Texas, a mob of Whites went in search of an African American they believed was writing for the *Chicago Defender.* The mob went on a rampage through the black community, burning and shooting up homes, beating blacks, and chasing them out of town.

White mobs took over Washington, DC, for four days, giving vent to their hatred and taking the lives of both Blacks and Whites.

One of the most violent race riots took place in Chicago, Illinois. A black youth swimming off the beach of Lake Michigan drowned when Whites began throwing stones because he was swimming in the area claimed for

Whites. The incident set off several days of rioting. Before the troops restored order, twenty-three African Americans and fifteen Whites were killed, hundreds were injured, and over one thousand families lost their homes.

THE DECADE OF THE 1920's

1920 The African American population was 10,463,131, or 9.9 percent of the U.S. population.

The Harlem Renaissance, a period of African American artistic and literary creativity, began. The period evolved through stages and resulted in an unprecedented output of creativity in art, literature, and theatre. This period lasted through the 1940's.

The first international convention of Marcus Garvey's Universal Improvement Association was held in Harlem on August 1.

1922 As the United States Congress debated an antilynching bill sponsored by Leonidas Dyer of Missouri, the NAACP took out a full page ad in the *New York Times* informing the public that 3,436 lynchings had occurred between 1889 and 1922, including 83 women. The bill, which had been killed by a filibuster in 1921, was hotly debated and passed in the House of Representatives in 1922. However, a well-organized southern filibuster in the Senate led to the defeat of the bill. A group of 24 governors, 39 mayors, 48 lawyers and justices, 3 archbishops, 83 bishops, and others had urged the approval of the bill.

1920 Two black general superintendents (the church refused to designate Blacks as bishops) were elected to serve in the United States. On May 19 Rev. Robert Elijah Jones was elected. Bishop Jones was born in Greensboro, North Carolina, and graduated from Bennett College and Gammon Theological Seminary. He had spent sixteen years as the editor of the *Southwestern Christian Advocate*. The day after Rev. Jones was elected, May 20, Rev. Matthew W. Clair, Sr., was elected. Although four black bishops had been elected previously, these two were the first elected to serve in the United States.

The World

1923 According to the Department of Labor, almost 500,000 African Americans left the South in the year between October 1922 and October 1923.

The first million-selling record by an African American artist was Bessie Smith's *Downhearted Blues/Gulf Coast Blues*.

Paul Robeson, an African American lawyer who turned to acting, starred in *The Emperor Jones*.

1924 The Immigration Act limited the number of Blacks and other ethnic groups allowed to enter the United States.

The United Methodist Church

1923 The Lexington Conference was held in Indianapolis, Indiana. Bishop Robert E. Jones presided. This was the first time an African American bishop had presided over the conference. The minutes recorded 101 effective pastors, 15 probationers, 23 retired, and 2 supernunary.

Gulfside Assembly, a Christian education retreat center for Blacks in Waveland, Mississippi, was founded by Bishop Robert. E. Jones. This was a unique and visionary project. It remains the only institution in The United Methodist Church founded and mostly supported by African Americans. Ravaged by hurricane and fire, Gulfside has survived and has remained true to its mission to serve the needs of people. It is a wonderful place for conferences, training, and spiritual retreats. Formerly, it served mostly black people, as it was the only large meeting place for black people. Now the center serves people of many diverse heritages. Gulfside is the burial site for Bishop and Mrs. Robert E. Jones.

1924 The General Conference adopted the name change from Freedmen's Aid Society to Board of Education for Negroes within the Board of Education. Southern Whites had accomplished their goal of diminishing the work and titlement of the Freedmen's Aid Society for The Methodist Episcopal Church for work with African Americans while controlling the resources of the church to enhance their segregated structures.

The World

1925 A. Philip Randolph founded the Brotherhood of Sleeping Car Porters (BSCP), the first successful African American trade union. The union secured better wages and working hours for the employees of the Pullman Palace Car Company, the largest employer of African Americans in the 1920's. The union also played a significant role in the fight for fair employment practices in other industries and was actively involved in the civil rights movement. When the union first formed, only about 1,900 of the 10,000 African American porters joined. They faced intimidation by the company as well as resistance from African Americans who were satisfied with the company's own union, which had been established to prevent the company's employees from forming other unions but did little to improve working conditions. Randolph and others were persuasive and received support from the NAACP, but it was not until the Railway Labor Act was passed in 1934 that Pullman was forced to recognize the BSCP.

1926 Negro History Week was established and celebrated for the first time. The celebration later developed into Black History Month, with focus on the history, contributions, and achievements of Blacks. February was chosen for Black History Month because it was the birth month of both Abraham Lincoln and Frederick Douglass.

The Carnegie Corporation purchased Arthur A. Schomburg's collection of books, documents, and artifacts about black history and donated it to the

The United Methodist Church

1925 Bradenton, Florida, was the site of the formation of the South Florida Conference on January 22.

1926 Laura Lange, Lexington Conference, was the first black woman ordained deacon by a bishop in The Methodist Episcopal Church. Ordained elder in 1936 by Bishop Matthew W. Clair, Sr., Laura Lange pastored several years in Kentucky.

Negro Division of the New York Library. In 1911 Schomburg and John E. Bruce had formed the Negro Society for Historical Research.

1927 James Weldon Johnson created a major work, a collection of poetry titled *God's Trombones*.

1928 Oscar DePriest from Chicago became the first African American elected to Congress since Reconstruction, taking office in 1929. He was chosen to run after an incumbent died during the campaign. DePriest was active in Chicago politics and delivered black votes for the Republican party. Among his successes in Congress was a bill to prohibit the federal Civilian Conservation Corp from discriminating in hiring and to increase appropriations to Howard University.

1929 On January 15, Dr. Martin Luther King, Jr., was born in Atlanta, Georgia.

The crash of the stock market led to economic disaster, and the world was plunged into a depression.

1928 The Southwest Conference organized at McGhee, Arkansas.

Friendship Homes were established in a number of cities as homes for Negro girls. They offered safe housing, child care, and nutrition programs. Open to young girls coming from rural areas or small towns, these homes were operated by The Methodist Episcopal Church. The original home in Ohio was established by the women in the Lexington Conference. One was started in Philadelphia by the women in the Delaware Conference. There were five in all, with national headquarters in Cincinnati. Mrs. Hattie Hargis was elected head of the Bureau of Friendship Homes, becoming one of the longest tenured African American bureau secretaries for the Women's Home Missionary Society.

1929 The Central West Conference was organized in Kansas City, Missouri, by Bishop Matthew W. Clair, Sr.

THE DECADE OF THE 1930'S

1931 The Scottsboro case became one of international notoriety, consisting of several trials, convictions, and final pardons in 1976 by governor George Wallace. On March 25 nine African Americans ages 13 to 20 were taken from a train near Scottsboro, Alabama, and falsely accused of raping two white women. Eight of the men were sentenced to death, and the ninth defendant's trail ended in a mistrial. Although one of the women later refuted the charges, it was 1937 before charges were dropped and four of the men were released from prison. By the time they were pardoned in 1976, only one was alive to hear the news.

1932 The Tuskegee Institute study of untreated syphilis in the Negro male began under the auspices of the United States Public Health Service and the Tuskegee Institute in Macon County, Alabama. It involved 600 poor black men, 399 who had contracted syphilis and 201 who had no symptoms. Initially the study was to last for one year, but it lasted 40 years. The men with the disease were told only that they had "bad blood." When penicillin became available as a treatment in the 1940's, the drug was not administered to the men. They were forced to suffer the ravages of the disease so the doctors could study their symptoms to the point of death. The study was halted in 1972 when the public became aware of its existence.

1933 Franklin Delano Roosevelt took office as President of the United States during the worst economic depression of the country's history. African Americans were suffering, especially in the South, where landowners did not share farm subsidies with sharecroppers, and African Americans were frequently subject to evictions. Roosevelt's New Deal legislation initiated a number of job and social programs, but additional legislation had to be enacted prohibiting discrimination.

Roosevelt appointed a Federal Council on Negro Affairs, known informally as the Black Cabinet. Among the members were William H. Hastie, Robert C. Weaver, and Mary McLeod Bethune. Bethune was the founder and first president of the National Council of Negro Women.

The NAACP began to fight segregation through the courts. It filed suit against the University of North Carolina on behalf of Thomas Hocutt. The case was lost on a technicality because the president of a Negro college failed to certify the record of the plaintiff.

1934 Arthur Mitchell of Illinois was elected to the United States Congress as the first African American Democrat, defeating Republican Oscar DePriest.

1935 Mary McLeod Bethune became head of a division of the National Youth Administration, becoming the first African American woman to head a United States government office.

1934 Ethel Payne, distinguished journalist, graduated from Garrett Biblical Institute. She was the first African American woman to do so.

Our Developing Methodist Roots

The World

Dr. Percy Julian, an African American chemist, produced a synthetic drug that would treat glaucoma.

1936 Roosevelt was reelected as African Americans shifted votes to Democrats.

The National Negro Congress was established. Its goals included the establishment of antilynching laws, desegregation, and unions for black voters.

African American Jesse Owens won four Olympic gold medals in Berlin.

African American Joe Louis won the heavyweight boxing championship.

1938 The NAACP fought segregation through the courts by establishing its Legal Defense Fund.

In December, the Supreme Court ruled that states must provide equal educational facilities for Negroes within its boundaries. The plaintiff in the related case, Lloyd Gaines, disappeared in March of 1939 and was never located.

The United Methodist Church

1936 Alexander P. Shaw was elected bishop (general superintendent) on May 14.

Alexander P. Shaw

1938 Bishop Alexander P. Shaw presided at the 69th session of the Lexington Conference, in the historic Cory Church in Cleveland, Ohio. In the conference minutes, page 23, a certificate of ordination attests that Grace Keene Thomas, Emma Lee Eulen, and George T. Brown had completed the Local Pastors Study and were ordained on April 23. Listed as acceptable supply pastors were Elizabeth Cleveland, Laura J. Lange, Edna Lee, Mary E. Smith, and Mary E. Washington. Laura Lange is also listed on the page of the appointees as deployed to the Smithland-Grand Rivers parish. The minutes also identify the following special appointments: Matthew Clair, Jr., to serve as professor at Gammon Theological School, and M. L. Harris to serve as president of Philander Smith College. Both later became bishops.

The World

1939 First Lady Eleanor Roosevelt resigned from the Daughters of the American Revolution when the group refused to allow Marian Anderson to sing at the DAR hall in Washington, DC. First Lady Roosevelt then invited Anderson to perform at the Lincoln Memorial.

The United States Department of Justice established the Civil Liberties Unit.

The United Methodist Church

1939 On April 26 in Kansas City, Missouri, the Uniting Conference reunited The Methodist Episcopal Church, The Methodist Episcopal Church, South, and The Methodist Protestant Church. The Conference implemented the creation of five geographical regions: Northeastern, Southeastern, South Central, North Central, and Western.

The Uniting Conference created the Central Jurisdiction, which was the segregated gerrymandering of all African American congregations outside the boundaries of the Western Jurisdiction. (African American churches in the Western Jurisdiction were not a part of the Central Jurisdiction.) This measure has come to be known by many African Americans as the "sinful compromise" or "the crime of '39."

Doctrines and Discipline of The Methodist Church—1939 (The Methodist Publishing House) described the Central Jurisdiction this way:

> ¶ 26. *Article I.*—The Methodist Church in the United States of America shall have Jurisdictional Conferences made up as follows: . . . *Central*—The Negro Annual Conferences, the Negro Mission Conferences and Missions in the United States of America."

Thus, Blacks were the "sacrificial lambs for segregation," the cost paid to the South for being willing to reunite with the rest of the church.

The Methodist Episcopal Church voted 470 for and 83 against union. The Methodist Protestant Church voted 142 for and 83 against.

The North Mississippi Conference was the only annual conference failing to support the plan of union.

The rejection of the plan by African American delegates was absolutely clear. Of the forty-seven African American delegates, thirty-six voted against the plan while eleven abstained. After the vote, the General Conference stood to sing "We're Marching To Zion." The African Americans remained seated, and some cried.

The African American General Conference delegates met to set the boundaries of the annual conferences of the new Central Jurisdiction. Some conferences were compact; others covered several states. One example of a large conference was the Lexington Conference, which included

> the Negro work in the states of Kentucky, Ohio, Michigan, Indiana, Illinois, Wisconsin and Minnesota, except so much of the state of Illinois as is included in the Central West Conference, and except Whitley, Knox, Bell and Harlan Counties in Kentucky.
> (*The Daily Christian Advocate*, May 9, 1939; page 365.)

The action of the Uniting Conference created confusion among white Methodists until 1968, if not to date. There were the African Americans who remained with the Methodist Episcopal Church, who formed the African American conferences making up the Central Jurisdiction. Then there were the African Americans in the African Methodist Episcopal Church (AME) and the African Methodist Episcopal Zion Church (AMEZ), both of which had churches in the territory that the Central Jurisdiction covered, and the Colored Methodist Episcopal Church (CME), which had formed in 1870. With the segregated structure, it was easy for southern Whites to forget that there were black "family members."

Assigning the right to elect bishops at the jurisdictional level enabled African Americans to elect their own leadership.

The Women's Division of Christian Service was established as part of the Board of Missions and Church Extensions, but it was granted authority to conduct its own business. The women had successfully negotiated through all the structures of the three uniting bodies and were not about to let anyone dictate their business. Although the Central Jurisdiction would have its own Women's Society of Christian Service and Wesleyan Service Guild, the women determined that their work would not be done in isolation.

An interim committee of African American women from the conferences of the Central Jurisdiction met at Clark College in Atlanta.

THE DECADE OF THE 1940's

*T*his decade was dominated by the dynamics of World War II. People in Europe were fleeing Hitler and the Holocaust. Women were replacing men in occupations vacated because of the need for men to go to war.

After African Americans returned from war, they were not content to accept the status quo. They used the courts and other means to secure opportunities and rights. The Supreme Court decided that Blacks had the right to vote in primaries.

A president died in office, the vice president assumed the office, and the military was desegregated by presidential executive order.

Penicillin was brought into use to fight infections. Television debuted. The jitterbug was the dance craze.

The segregated status continued in the church. Within the Central Jurisdiction, leaders continued to set high expectations for mission and ministry, and significant growth was made.

1940

The Virginia legislature adopted "Carry Me Back to Ol' Virginny," by African American James A. Bland, as the state song.

Dr. Charles R. Drew, an African American physician and surgeon, discovered how to preserve blood plasma and helped to save many lives during the war. He became the director of the American Red Cross Blood Bank Program. Later he resigned in a dispute about the segregation of blood. He became professor of surgery at Howard University. Dr. Drew died in 1950 from injuries sustained in a car accident.

Benjamin O. Davis, Sr., became the first African American promoted to the rank of Brigadier General. The White House announcement was made October 25.

1940

At the first General Conference following the formation of The Methodist Church, the Committee on Special Days reported on funds raised on Race Relations Sunday to support African American colleges. The report included the line, "...and the CME Church." Objections were raised since the label "the CME Church" indicated a lack of understanding that the CME Church was a separate denomination and that the Central Jurisdiction, of whom the report was speaking, was a part of the The Methodist Church. Amendments were offered.

This insensitivity in the first General Conference set the tone for how African Americans in the Central Jurisdiction would fare. African Americans, it seems, would always have to explain why they stayed,

The National Negro Congress dissolved.

Hattie McDaniel became the first African American to win an Academy Award. She won for best supporting actress in *Gone With the Wind*.

why they remained loyal to a denomination that gave them little respect. While many left, yielding to pressure by black brothers and sisters who had left and by other independent denominations, approximately three hundred thousand African American Methodists stayed because they had been born into the church or had selected the church by choice, and they lived with the hope that the church would live out the mandates of the gospel and the ecclesiology of Wesley. They believed they had something to offer. African American Methodists were also appreciative of the way Methodists had reached out during slavery and after the Civil War, with an emphasis on education. Many felt that they would rather work within for reform than have no voice outside.

Union Memorial Methodist Church in St. Louis, Missouri, was the site of the organizing session of the Central Jurisdiction. By the time of this meeting two months after the General Conference, the impact of the church's decision had sunk in, and the leaders went about ordering the business of the Jurisdiction.

Election of bishops was one of the important and exciting tasks to be completed. On the second ballot, W.A.C. Hughes was elected. He was from the Washington Annual Conference and was the Secretary of Colored Work of the Board of Home Missions and Church Extension. Unfortunately, Bishop Hughes died less than a month after his election.

On the fifth ballot of the fourth morning, Lorenzo Houston King was elected. Dr. King was the pastor of St. Mark Methodist Church in

The World

1941 President Roosevelt, yielding to pressure from A. Philip Randolph and other civil rights leaders who were organizing 100,000 African Americans to march on Washington, issued Executive Order 8802, creating the Fair Employment Practices Committee and banning discrimination in defense industries, government training programs, and war industries. When the order was executed, Randolph called off the scheduled march.

The U.S. Army's first flying school for black cadets was opened in Tuskegee, Alabama.

The United Methodist Church

New York. The New York Conference was not a part of the Central Jurisdiction, thus a significant statement was made by this action!

A provisional committee of the Central Jurisdiction women met with delegates from the nineteen annual conferences at the same time that the Central Jurisdiction met. Board of Missions members for the 1940–1944 quadrennium were elected, and advisory members were chosen.

In December the charter meeting of the Central Jurisdiction's Women's Society of Christian Service (WSCS) took place at Calvary Methodist Church in Cincinnati, Ohio. On the evening of December 9, one of the speakers was Dr. Mary McLeod Bethune, president of Bethune-Cookman College in Daytona Beach, Florida. Dr. Bethune was widely known for her activism. She was an advisor to the White House and founder of the National Council of Negro Women. Dr. Bethune was one of the spiritual mothers of the WSCS. She served in the Women's Division.

Dorie Miller, an African American sailor on the USS *Arizona*, took over an unmanned machine gun during the Pearl Harbor attack, bringing down as many as four enemy planes. He was eventually awarded the Navy Cross for his actions.

The United States entered World War II.

1942
The Congress of Racial Equality (CORE) was founded in Chicago, Illinois, by a group of African Americans and Whites who believed in nonviolent resistance. CORE conducted the first sit-ins, protesting discrimination in Chicago restaurants. The national organization was established one year later.

1943
George Washington Carver died in Tuskegee, Alabama, January 5. Carver was a former slave who became an agricultural scientist and revolutionized the southern agricultural economy with his discovery of hundreds of products that could be derived from the peanut and the sweet potato.

William H. Hastie resigned from his position as civilian aide to the Secretary of War on January 5 in protest against the Army's policy of segregation and discrimination.

A number of race riots occurred:
- Mobile, Alabama—There were disputes over the upgrading of twelve African American workers in the shipyards. Troops were called in.

- Beaumont, Texas—Martial law was declared.
- Detroit, Michigan—Thirty-four people died. Military police were sent in to restore order.
- Harlem, New York—Riots started after a white policeman shot a black soldier.

1944 In the case *Smith* v. *Allwright*, the Supreme Court banned the white primary, established by some southern states to prohibit voting by African Americans.

African Americans were commissioned as U.S. Navy officers for the first time, and two naval vessels had crews largely composed of African Americans.

The United Negro College Fund was incorporated on April 25.

Adam Clayton Powell, Jr., became the first African American congressman elected from the East.

African American sculptor Selma Burke designed the portrait of Franklin Roosevelt that is used on the dime.

1944 The General Conference enacted legislation (a constitutional revision) making Liberia a part of the Central Jurisdiction. It remained in this relationship for twenty years.

The Methodist Church adopted "Crusade for Christ" as the Quadrennial Program, and the Central Jurisdiction's share of the $25 million goal to be raised was $796,300.

The Second Central Jurisdictional Conference elected its bishops. Willis J. King, president of Gammon Theological Seminary, was elected to serve Liberia. Others elected were Robert N. Brooks, editor of the *Central Christian Advocate*, and Edward W. Kelly, pastor of Union Memorial Church in St. Louis.

Willis J. King

Bishop Robert E. Jones retired after twenty-four years of service. The Conference also acknowledged the death of Bishop Matthew W. Clair, Sr.

The World

The United Methodist Church

1945 On September 2 the Japanese signed surrender documents. An estimated 1,154,720 African Americans had been inducted or drafted into the armed services.

On September 18 one thousand white students from three schools in Gary, Indiana, protested school integration by staging a walk-out.

Ebony magazine began publication.

African American poet Gwendolyn Brooks published her first book of poems, *A Street in Bronzeville.*

1946 On June 3 the Supreme Court ruled that laws requiring segregation in interstate bus travel were invalid.

Race riots in Columbia, Tennessee, left two people dead and ten wounded. In Athens, Alabama, an estimated fifty to one hundred African Americans were injured in riots.

President Harry S. Truman created the President's Committee on Civil Rights by Executive Order 9808 on December 5.

1947 Jackie Robinson played his first game for the Brooklyn Dodgers, breaking the color barrier in major league baseball. Jackie won Rookie of the Year.

The first Freedom Riders, organized by CORE, rode public interstate transportation in the South to test the application of court rulings against segregation.

The World

On September 21, Archbishop Joseph E. Ritter issued an edict stating that he would excommunicate any Catholics involved in lawsuits to stop the integration of St. Louis's parochial schools.

"An Appeal to the World," the NAACP petition on racial injustices in America, was formally presented to the United Nations at Lake Success, New York, on October 23.

On October 29 the President's Committee on Civil Rights issued a formal report entitled "To Secure These Rights," which condemned discrimination against African Americans.

From Slavery to Freedom: A History of American Negros, by John Hope Franklin, was published.

1948
A Supreme Court decision in *Sipuel* v. *The Board of Regents of the University of Oklahoma* held that states must provide law schools for Negroes as soon they provided law schools for Whites.

President Harry S. Truman issued Executive Order 9981 to integrate the armed forces. The order mandated "equality of treatment and opportunity" in the armed forces. His administration failed to win congressional passage of civil rights legislation.

South Africa began the apartheid system of legally mandated racial segregation.

The United Methodist Church

1948
The General Conference voted that Crusade Scholarships would include ethnic minorities who planned to become full-time Christian workers.

At the General Conference, the report showed that the church's goal of $25 million for Crusade for Christ had been exceeded, with actual receipts of $27,011,243. The Central Jurisdiction contributed $770,330, and seven Central Jurisdiction conferences paid their apportionments in full.

Many Methodists were sensing the tensions in the secular culture as change was coming. Segregation was being attacked. The first freedom

The World

Edward R. Dudley became the first African American to be appointed as a United States ambassador. He was the ambassador to Liberia until 1953.

On September 18 the United Nations Security Council confirmed African American Ralph J. Bunche as acting United Nations mediator in Palestine.

On October 1 the California Supreme Court ruled that the state statute banning interracial marriage violated the constitution.

1949 Congressman William L. Dawson from Chicago, Illinois, was approved as chairman of the House Expenditures Committee, becoming the first African American to chair a standing committee of Congress. Dawson was elected to Congress in 1942 and held the seat until his retirement in 1970. He was a magna cum laude graduate of Fisk University and earned a law degree at Northwestern University.

The United Methodist Church

rides had taken place in 1947. Members of Methodist churches were participating in the activism. How long would the church be immune to direct action?

In the meeting of the Central Jurisdiction in Atlanta, Georgia, a motion was made and passed to form a Commission to Study the Central Jurisdiction, and for the commission to report back to the Central Jurisdictional Conference in 1952.

Bishop J.W.E. Bowen was elected as the sixth bishop of the Central Jurisdiction.

J. Ernest Wilkins was appointed to the Judicial Council of The Methodist Church. In 1956 he became president of the Judicial Council, the first African American to serve in that position.

Theresa Hoover, an African American woman from Arkansas, became a field worker for the Women's Division of the Board of Global Ministries, where she served for ten years.

On June 3 Wesley A. Brown became the first African American to graduate from the United States Naval Academy.

WERD, the first radio station owned by an African American, began broadcasting in Atlanta, Georgia, on October 7.

Gordon Parks became the first African American photographer to work on the *Life* magazine staff.

THE DECADE OF THE 1950's

*W*orld War II had ended, and thousands of servicemen returned home. African Americans who had fought for their country returned expecting their country to treat them better. Industrialization was underway, creating jobs and new communities. Continued threats of war led to the building of bomb shelters, drills in schools, and civil defense plans. Production of the hydrogen bomb was approved. Fears of Communism escalated. Dr. Jonas Salk developed the first polio vaccine. Television continued to gain popularity and soon brought mass media into homes.

1950 April was a month of sorrow as African Americans lost three giants to death: Dr. Charles R. Drew, Dr. Carter G. Woodson, and Attorney Charles H. Houston. Houston was the first chief legal counsel of the NAACP, Vice Dean of Howard University Law School, and mentor of the young Thurgood Marshall.

On June 5, three Supreme Court decisions undermined the legal structure of segregation. In the Sweatt case, the Court held that equality involved more than physical facilities. In the McLaurin case, the Court held that a student, once admitted, could not be segregated. In the Henderson case, the Court ruled against "curtains, partitions and signs" that separated African American dining car patrons from Whites.

Gwendolyn Brooks received a Pulitzer Prize for her book of poetry, *Annie Allen*, becoming the first African American author to win a Pulitzer Prize.

On June 27 President Truman ordered United States armed forces into the Korean conflict.

On December 10 United Nations official Ralph J. Bunche received the Nobel Peace Prize for mediating the Palestine crisis and negotiating a truce in the first Arab and Israeli War. He went on to serve the United Nations in various capacities all over the world.

1951
W.E.B. DuBois's work with the International Peace Movement, his international travels, and his outspokenness against injustices in the United States led to his being accused of Communism and falling prey to the McCarthy anti-Communist witch hunt. The United States revoked his passport.

The NAACP zoomed onto segregation and discrimination at elementary schools and high schools and argued cases in U.S. district courts in South Carolina and Kansas. The South Carolina court ruled 2-1 (dissenting voice by Judge J. Waties Waring) that segregation was not discrimination. The Kansas court ruled that the separate facilities at issue were equal but that segregation per se had an adverse effect on African American children. These two cases were later combined with others into *Brown* v. *Board of Education*.

The University of North Carolina admitted the first African American student in its 162-year history.

The Washington, DC, Municipal Court of Appeals ruled that segregation in restaurants was illegal.

A bill passed by the New York City Council prohibited racial discrimination in city-assisted housing.

The U.S. Army deactivated the 24th Infantry Regiment during the Korean War and integrated its members into other regiments. The 24th was the last of the segregated units activated by Congress in 1866.

President Truman created a committee to supervise compliance with provisions against discrimination by contractors and subcontractors with the U.S. government.

Harry T. Moore, Florida coordinator for the NAACP, was killed by a bomb in his home in Mims, Florida, on December 25. His wife was severely injured and died days later.

1952 The University of Tennessee in Knoxville admitted its first African American student in January.

Tindley Temple. See 1864 on page 55, and 1952 on page 93.

1952 There was growing advocacy for desegregation of The Methodist Church.

The World

The novel *Invisible Man*, by African American Ralph Ellison, was published. It went on to win the National Book Award.

There were eight African American gold medalists at the Olympic Games in Helsinki.

The Tuskegee Institute announced on December 30 that for the first time in seventy-one years of record keeping, no lynchings were reported during that year.

1953 The Supreme Court ruled that District of Columbia restaurants could not legally refuse to serve African Americans.

The integration of the previously all-white Trumbull Park housing project in Chicago precipitated persistent violence against African Americans who moved in there. The violence continued for years. Large numbers of police were assigned to protect the African Americans.

The fighting in Korea was ended.

1954 On May 17, in a historic landmark decision, the U.S. Supreme Court ruled that segregation in public schools was unconstitutional, overturning the doctrine of "separate but equal" that had prevailed since the *Plessey* v. *Ferguson* decision. This case, *Brown* v. *Board of Education*,

The United Methodist Church

Sentiment within the church seemed to be growing to welcome African American churches within the geographical jurisdictions.

On June 18 the Central Jurisdiction convened at Tindley Temple Methodist Church in Philadelphia, Pennsylvania. Two bishops were elected: Edgar A. Love and Matthew Wesley Clair, Jr.

Dr. James P. Brawley presented the report of the Commission to Study the Central Jurisdiction that had been appointed by the 1948 conference of the Central Jurisdiction. The report was adopted and the commission was extended for another quadrennium.

Edgar A. Love

1954 J. Ernest Wilkins, an active lay member of St. Mark Methodist Church in Chicago, Illinois, was named Assistant Secretary of Labor by President Dwight Eisenhower. Wilkins had previously served on the Committee on Government Contracts. He

was presented and argued by NAACP chief legal counsel Thurgood Marshall. Although the case was about denying Linda Brown attendance at the white school near her home, the lawsuit actually combined four class action lawsuits from Kansas, South Carolina, Virginia, and Delaware. This decision changed public education in the country, but segregationists in the South and in the North would not accept the decision without overt and covert racist behaviors from different arenas of leadership.

In Indianola, Mississippi, opponents of integration organized the first White Citizens Council.

School integration took place in Washington, DC, and Baltimore, Maryland, when schools opened in September.

Benjamin O. Davis, Jr., became the first African American Air Force general.

The Defense Department announced the end of the last African American unit in the U.S. armed forces.

1955 Mary McLeod Bethune died on May 18.

Marian Anderson sang at the Metropolitan Opera House, the first African American in the company's history to do so.

The Supreme Court ruled that school integration must take place "with all deliberate speed."

was the first African American to occupy a subcabinet post. He had earlier served in the military in World War I and practiced law in Chicago.

When fourteen-year-old African American Emmett Till was visiting his uncle in Mississippi, he allegedly whistled at a white woman. He was kidnapped, brutalized, shot, and thrown in the river. His naked and mutilated body was found three days later. Although Roy Bryant and his half brother admitted kidnapping Emmett, the all-white jury acquitted them. Emmett's mother in Chicago insisted on an open casket so that the world could see what was done to her son. This tragedy rallied the cause for a renewed civil rights movement. The pictures shown around the world and the outrage expressed ensured that provision for federal investigations into civil rights violations would be included in the Civil Rights Act of 1957.

The Interstate Commerce Commission banned segregation in interstate transportation and travel facilities.

On December 1, Rosa Parks, a seamstress, boarded a bus in Montgomery, Alabama. She sat one seat in front of the "colored section" and refused to move when more Whites boarded. Three other Blacks moved, but Parks did not. Police were called and Rosa was arrested, igniting the community. The Montgomery Bus Boycott was born when the Women's Political Council, led by JoAnn Robinson, initiated the idea of a one-day boycott on the day Parks was to appear in court. Public buses were almost totally void of black people on that day. After Parks was convicted, area black leaders met to consider further action and formed the Montgomery Improvement Association, to be led by the new pastor in town, Rev. Martin Luther King, Jr. The association planned a sustained public transportation boycott that would end up lasting over a year (see 1956). Rosa Parks became known as "the mother of civil rights."

1956
The home of Dr. Martin Luther King, Jr., was bombed. He and his family escaped injury.

Autherine J. Lucy was admitted to the University of Alabama Graduate School as its first African American student on February 3. After a riot occurred at the school, she was suspended on February 7 and subsequently expelled on February 29. The expulsion was overruled in 1988, and Lucy returned to school and earned a master's degree in education in 1992.

Nearly one hundred southern members of Congress issued a declaration that became known as the Southern Manifesto, protesting the Supreme Court's decision banning segregation in public schools.

Singer Nat "King" Cole was attacked by racists while on stage in Birmingham, Alabama. Later, near the end of the year, Cole began hosting his own nationwide television variety show.

A white mob in Mansfield, Texas, prevented African American students from enrolling in the local high school.

The National Guard was sent to Clinton, Tennessee, to stop mob protests against the integration of schools.

1956
Dr. Willa Beatrice Player was installed as the tenth president of Bennett College in Greensboro, North Carolina, where she served until 1966. She was the first female black president of any four-year school in the country. During Dr. Player's administration, Bennett became one of the first African American colleges to be admitted into the membership of the Southern Association of Colleges and Schools. Dr. Player was a strong supporter of Dr. Martin Luther King, Jr.

The General Conference of The Methodist Church met in Minneapolis, Minnesota, in April. Amidst the cultural changes taking place in the country regarding desegregation, voting and rights, and political shifts, the church was at a critical time. Growing numbers were dissatisfied with a segregated church.

A resolution was introduced asking for the study of the jurisdictional system and recommended actions. The resolution did not specifically name the Central Jurisdiction, but many were hopeful that once the topic was opened there would be no way to avoid the racially segregated jurisdiction. The resolution to form a Commission to Study and Recommend Action Concerning the Jurisdictional System was passed and referred to the Committee on Conferences.

The World

The Montgomery, Alabama, public transportation boycott born from Rosa Parks's arrest continued. On June 5 a federal court declared that forced segregation on city buses in Montgomery was unconstitutional. On November 13 the Supreme Court upheld this decision. Federal injunctions were served to force local and state officials to comply with the ruling. After another Supreme Court decision upheld a lower court ruling forbidding segregated bus seating, and after more than a year of boycotting, the boycott was called off and, on December 21, African Americans began using the now-integrated buses.

In Birmingham on Christmas day, a bomb destroyed the home of Rev. F. L. Shuttlesworth, a leader in the fight against segregation.

1957

After an initial meeting in Atlanta, the Southern Leadership Conference was more formally organized in a February meeting in New Orleans. The group elected Martin Luther King, Jr., as its president. The group's name was modified in August to the Southern Christian Leadership Conference.

The Prayer Pilgrimage for Freedom took place in Washington, DC, on May 17. It was the largest demonstration by African Americans up to that time.

The Civil Rights Act of 1957 was signed into law, reinforcing voting rights guaranteed by the fifteenth amendment. It was the first civil rights bill passed by Congress since 1875.

The United Methodist Church

Another significant resolution was introduced on May 3. It provided for an amendment to the Constitution (Amendment IX), leading to the dissolution of the Central Jurisdiction. The amendment provided for the voluntary transfer of churches into annual conferences of the geographical jurisdictions by mutual agreement of the two conferences involved. It was a lengthy and complex process.

J. Ernest Wilkins became president of the Judicial Council, the first African American to lead that group.

Prince Albert Taylor, Jr., an African American, was elected bishop.

Prince Albert Taylor, Jr.

Nine African American students enrolled in Central High School in Little Rock, Arkansas. Riots ensued, and President Dwight D. Eisenhower ordered federal troops to prevent obstruction of the school's integration. President Eisenhower went on television and radio to explain that he had sent troops in with reluctance after the governor, Orval Faubus, had challenged the authority of the federal government. Daisy Bates was an NAACP official shepherding "the Little Rock Nine" in the historic endeavor. Millions were able to see on television the hatred in the contorted faces of Whites, male and female, as they harassed school children.

1958 Dr. Martin Luther King, Jr., published his first book, *Stride Toward Freedom*. Later that month, while autographing books in Harlem, he was stabbed by a mentally ill African American woman.

1959 Lorraine Hansberry's play *A Raisin in the Sun* opened, starring Sydney Poitier and Claudia McNeal. It was the first play written by an African American woman to reach Broadway and the first directed by an African American in half a century.

Mack Parker, accused of rape, was dragged from a jail cell, shot, and lynched in Poplarville, Mississippi.

Prince Edward County in Virginia closed all of its public schools in order to avoid integration.

1958 Sallie Crenshaw, a member of the former East Tennessee Conference, was the first African American woman ordained elder and admitted into full connection in an annual conference of The Methodist Church.

THE DECADE OF THE 1960's

The decade of the sixties was nation-altering as Black America experienced discontent with the segregated and discriminatory society in which they lived. The civil rights movement took on different dimensions, often pitting various black groups against each other and certainly expanding on a generational divide. Bold protests, sit-ins, and emergence of a growing number of young people who were less content to accept the staus quo and more willing to take direct action set the nation on a different course. The NAACP filed a number of lawsuits. Demonstrations moved from college campuses and public facilities to elementary schools, where young mothers and other citizens demonstrated.

White America was experiencing young people not wanting to live under the conservative rubric of their parents. Some young white people got involved in the civil rights movement; others got involved in religious groups or cults, hippie movements, and other nonmainstream activities. Indeed, changes were taking place and moving too slowly for some and too fast for others.

This book does not include the stories of individual church members or conference congregations participating directly and indirectly in sit-ins, freedom rides, marches, voter registration, and other means to advance equality in this country. But those stories are in the pages and memories of local churches and annual conferences.

The major institutions and lifestyles of this nation education, employment, law enforcement, law, medicine, and others were undergoing significant changes. And the church was not exempt! The Methodist Church was practicing its own segregation by having a church within a church, but there were activists within the church who were challenging her to get her house in order. The church had to be pushed. It was not sounding a prophetic word to its members about their behaviors in front of schools, about their plantation-run farms, about their resistance to federal laws. Methodist congregations were even refusing to allow African Americans in to worship! Challenges were being made about the hiring policies of church agencies and boards.

The Hispanic population tripled during the decade and began its own advocacy for rights.

1960 On February 1 four African American students from North Carolina A and T College walked into a Woolworth's in

1960 The General Conference met in Denver, Colorado. The report of the Commission to Study and Recommend

The World

Greensboro, North Carolina, and sat down at the lunch counter. No one came to serve them, and they sat there quietly all afternoon. For the next several days they came and brought other students with them. The sit-in movement was not new, but this time college students and other young people brought a new determination to make a difference. Soon sit-ins were sweeping the South. Sometimes the demonstrators were spat on, cursed, and harassed. Sometimes they were hauled away to jail, but they kept coming! As spring approached, many churches urged congregations to do without Easter shopping, and economic boycotts were added to the protests. Nashville, Tennessee, department stores lost forty percent of their retail sales when African Americans curtailed their shopping.

Since most of the sit-ins were being organized on college campuses, the demonstrators were teenagers and young people. While many elders were alarmed (when they knew), they supported their kids. The NAACP, CORE, and the Southern Christian Leadership Conference all gave the movement their support. In April the students formed their own organization, the Student Nonviolent Coordinating Committee (SNCC).

In February, police arrested nearly one hundred students at a sit-in in Nashville.

On March 1, hundreds (perhaps as many as one thousand) of Alabama State students demonstrated at the state capital. The next day, the Board of Education expelled nine of the students.

The United Methodist Church

Action Concerning the Jurisdictional System was presented. The report offered no recommendation for any change in the Central Jurisdiction. Leaders from the Central Jurisdiction were disappointed that there was neither a specific plan of inclusion nor a timeline by which the Central Jurisdiction would be abolished.

During the course of debate about the report and about other issues of race, a delegate from North Carolina, Edwin L. Jones, offered a resolution to abolish the Central Jurisdiction and divide the churches in the jurisdiction between the Northeastern and North Central Jurisdictions. The resolution generated much debate but was defeated.

Charles Franklin Golden   Noah Watson Moore, Jr.   Marquis LaFayette Harris

Cory Methodist Church in Cleveland, Ohio, was the site of the 1960 Central Jurisdictional Conference. Three bishops were elected: Charles Franklin Golden, Noah Watson Moore, Jr., and Marquis LaFayette Harris.

The World

The Associated Press reported on March 22 that more than one thousand African Americans had been arrested in sit-in demonstrations.

In Nashville, Tennessee, a bomb destroyed much of the home of attorney Z. Alexander Looby on April 19. Looby was defending many of the students arrested for participating in sit-ins. An estimated four thousand African Americans marched to city hall to protest the bombing.

In May, the Civil Rights Act of 1960 was signed into law by President Eisenhower.

African American Wilma Rudolph won three gold medals at the Olympics in Rome. In order to celebrate her accomplishments, her hometown of Clarksville, Tennessee, had to desegregate its facilities. Clarksville proudly boasts of its Wilma Rudolph Boulevard.

In October, four national chain stores announced that counters in about 150 stores had been integrated. The stores were located in 112 cities in Florida, Kentucky, Maryland, Missouri, North Carolina, Oklahoma, Tennessee, Texas, Virginia, and West Virginia. The trend continued through other cities.

African Americans' votes were a significant factor in the election of John F. Kennedy as President of the United States.

The United Methodist Church

The Central Jurisdictional Conference authorized a Committee of Five to study the Central Jurisdiction. While the work of the committee was broadly interpreted to work with any agencies, commissions, or persons whose goal was the inclusion of the Central Jurisdiction, the strategy was clearly for the committee to have input into any plans to include or dissolve the Central Jurisdiction.

In November, members of the Committee of Five were named: Richard C. Erwin of the Baltimore Area, a layman and lawyer; Rev. John H. Graham of the Nashville-Birmingham Area, a staff member of the General Board of Missions; William Astor Kirk of the New Orleans Area, a layman and staff member of the General Board of Christian Social Concerns; Rev. John J. Hicks of the St. Louis area, pastor of Union Memorial Church; and Rev. James S. Thomas of the Atlantic Coast area, a staff member of the General Board of Education.

African American Adam Clayton Powell, who had much support in New York's Harlem, became chairman of the Education and Labor Committee of the House of Representatives.

1961

SNCC promoted a Southwide jail-in movement where students refused to pay fines and were sent to jail, thereby overcrowding jails.

Robert Weaver became administrator of the U.S. Housing and Home Finance Agency. This was the highest post an African American had ever held in the U.S. Government.

African Americans and white leaders in Atlanta, Georgia, met to develop plans for desegregation of lunchrooms, public facilities, and Atlanta's high schools.

Freedom bus riders began a series of trips through the South to test the federal regulations regarding interstate travel. Some riders were arrested; some were mobbed by angry segregationists. In some instances buses were bombed. United States marshals were ordered into some states.

Civil unrest was occurring across the country. Many people from the North, Whites as well as African Americans, went south to join in demonstrations and protests. Numerous church people were involved in the witness. Police were as much of a problem as others at these events. They used tear gas and unleashed dogs on the demonstrators.

The World

African American Leontyne Price made her opera debut at the Metropolitan Opera House, where she wowed audiences. Leontyne, who had two Methodist grandfathers, began her musical life at an early age in St. Paul Methodist Church in Laurel, Mississippi. Her mother took her to see Marian Anderson when she was nine years old. She was impressed and inspired, and the rest became history. Leontyne became an internationally acclaimed diva.

1962 Demonstrations and protests continued. Waves of terror reigned throughout the South as Whites engaged in bombings, attacks, and assaults. In Georgia alone, eight churches were burned, including churches in Leesburg, Sasser, Dawson, and Macon.

Archbishop Joseph Rummel excommunicated three people when they persisted in opposing his decision to integrate Catholic schools in New Orleans.

In response to church burnings, African American leaders beseeched the federal government to halt the reign of terror in Georgia.

African Americans engaged in voter registration in Mississippi found themselves fired upon and harassed.

African American James Meredith, a veteran, attempted to enroll in the University of Mississippi. He was blocked by the defiant governor Ross Barnett. Supreme Court Justice Hugo Black vacated the ruling of a circuit

The United Methodist Church

1962 The Cincinnati Exploratory Meeting was convened in Cincinnati March 26–28. The College of Bishops of the Central Jurisdiction called for this meeting to gather information about the differing views and feelings of people at the grassroots level about the many issues surrounding the inclusion or elimination of the Central Jurisdiction.

court judge and ordered the university to admit Meredith. Governor Barnett defied the government, but a federal circuit court ordered the Board of Higher Education of Mississippi to admit Meredith. The court's orders were again defied. The governor and the lieutenant governor were found in contempt, and fines were assessed. Meredith began classes, and federal marshals were assigned to escort him. The President had to enlist the assistance of the National Guard before Meredith was finally registered. A former major general of the United States Army was arrested for inciting insurrection by recruiting volunteers to defy the federal government and encouraging students to engage in rioting on campus.

Jackie Robinson was inducted into the Baseball Hall of Fame, the first African American to be included there.

1963
In celebration of the emancipation centennial, massive voter education and registration workshops and campaigns were conducted across the South.

Unemployment among African Americans was as high as it had been during the Great Depression.

Hope for things getting better was getting dim in spite of a number of individual achievements. Urban cities in the North were experiencing problems as ghettos spread, crowding schools. Invisible boundaries of limitations were imposed.

The World

Antisegregation campaigns continued. Homes of antisegregation leaders and churches continued to be targets of the segregationists.

In Birmingham, Alabama, police attacked civil rights marchers with high-power water hoses and guns. Nationally televised news showing the scenes not only stirred the nation but created problems for parents when young children raised questions about treatment of black people. African Americans in families where members were of differing hues had to answer questions about race that heretofore were unnecessary.

In a historic radio and television address, President John F. Kennedy described segregation as morally wrong and appealed to local and state legislatures and Congress to outlaw remaining laws of segregation. He also appealed to individuals to act responsibly in their daily lives.

Medgar Evers, field secretary for the NAACP in Mississippi, was shot down in the driveway of his home. His wife, Myrlie, heard the shot and ran outside to him. He died in a hospital less than an hour later. Byron De La Beckwith, a white racist, bragged about his deed. It took three trials and thirty years before a conviction was rendered.

The March on Washington, organized by A. Philip Randolph and others, drew an estimated 250,000 participants to the nation's capital. Dr. Martin Luther King, Jr., delivered his famous "I Have a Dream" speech. During the series of speeches, Roy Wilkins, Executive Secretary of the NAACP,

The United Methodist Church

announced the death of Dr. W.E.B. DuBois, who had died the previous night in Ghana.

In Birmingham, Alabama, on a Sunday morning, four African American girls died when the Sixteenth Street Baptist Church was bombed. Addie Mae Collins, Denise McNair, Carole Robertson, and Cynthia Wesley were young innocents who should not have had to pay the ultimate price for freedom. This tragedy occurred barely two weeks after Dr. King's speech in Washington. African Americans expressed their anger about the bombings in the streets. It was not until 2002 that the last of the guilty was convicted. Ironically, the identity of the guilty was known immediately because their group had been infiltrated by government agents. When this became public, the anger of African Americans was rekindled.

John F. Kennedy, President of the United States, was assassinated in Dallas, Texas, on November 22. He was 46 years old.

1964 Dr. Martin Luther King, Jr., was awarded the Nobel Peace Prize.

The Civil Rights Act of 1964 was passed by Congress when, for the first time, the Senate ended a southern filibuster by imposing cloture. President Lyndon B. Johnson signed the measure on July 2. The act outlawed discrimination in public accommodations, education, and employment. It was followed in August by the Economic Opportunity Act.

Demonstration for abolition of the Central Jurisdiction at the 1964 General Conference

1964 At the 1964 General Conference of The Methodist Church in Pittsburgh, Pennsylvania, the report of the Committee on Interjurisdictional Relations was presented in the first few days of the Conference. Amendments were offered by African Americans who had served on the committee. A lengthy debate ensued, though eventually the report was adopted.

The World

Three civil rights workers—James Earl Chaney, an African American, along with Andrew Goodman and Michael Schwerner, both white—disappeared while working in Mississippi for voter registration. President Johnson sent the FBI in to look for them, and for almost two months volunteers searched. They were found dead, buried in a shallow grave on a farm near Philadelphia, Mississippi. They had been arrested by a deputy sheriff and handed over to the Ku Klux Klan.

Fannie Lou Hamer and others under the banner of the Mississippi Freedom Democratic Party attempted to unseat the all-white Mississippi Democratic delegation at the National Convention. Hammer's famous statement, "I'm sick and tired of being sick and tired," remains a familiar quote among many African Americans expressing frustration at the slowness of justice.

Sidney Poitier became the first African American to win an Oscar for best actor for his performance in the movie *Lilies of the Field*.

Nelson Mandela was sentenced to life imprisonment for his activities in the fight to overthrow apartheid in South Africa.

The United Methodist Church

Bishop Prince A. Taylor returned from eight years in Liberia and was assigned to serve in New Jersey, an integrated conference.

The Central Jurisdiction met at Bethune-Cookman College in Daytona Beach, Florida. The report of the Committee of Five (to study the Central Jurisdiction) was presented by its chair, Rev. Dr. James S. Thomas. The report included a plan for realigning the conferences in the Central Jurisdiction with those in the geographical jurisdictions. The plan was adopted after debate and a round of amendments, most of which were rejected.

James S. Thomas

On the seventeenth ballot, James Samuel Thomas was elected Bishop. It was known that he would not serve in the Central Jurisdiction but would be transferred to the North Central Jurisdiction. In September he was assigned to the Iowa Area. Thus, he became the first African American bishop to serve in the North Central Jurisdiction.

The Delaware Annual Conference of the Central Jurisdiction was received in the Northeastern Jurisdiction of the general church without incident.

There was a mutually acceptable merger of the Lexington Annual Conference of the Central Jurisdiction and the North Central Jurisdiction of the general church.

1965

In Marion, Alabama, as African American Jimmy Lee Jackson and others were leaving a voting demonstration at a local church, they were attacked by police and state troopers. Jimmy Lee was shot as he tried to protect his mother and grandfather. He died eight days later. Dr. Martin Luther King, Jr., came to speak at his funeral. After the funeral a march was organized from Selma to Montgomery to protest at the capital. As the marchers got to the bridge leading out of Selma, they were attacked by state troopers. Television cameras captured the scene, and viewers around the world saw the vicious, bloody attack. Civil rights activists would hereafter refer to this day as Bloody Sunday. Two weeks later the march was begun again under the protection of federal marshals and troops, with religious leaders and citizens from across the country.

Viola Liuzzo, a white housewife and mother from Detroit, paid the ultimate price for her belief. After she witnessed the events on Bloody Sunday, she went to Alabama to assist in the movement and was murdered by Klansmen after transporting marchers back to Selma.

The Voting Rights Acts of 1965 was passed in August and signed into law by President Lyndon Johnson. The act banned literacy tests and other ruses the South had used to deny the vote to African Americans. The act also provided for oversight by Washington and sent federal examiners to the South to register voters.

The World

Malcolm X was assassinated after a break with the Nation of Islam and after a trip to Africa and Mecca changed his philosophy away from hatred and separatism and toward political involvement.

1966 Edward W. Brooke of Massachusetts was elected to the United States Senate. He was the first African American senator since the days of Reconstruction. Brooke graduated from Howard University with a degree in chemistry. He was an army captain and had practiced law, headed the Boston Finance Commission, and served as Attorney General for the state prior to being elected on the Republican ticket to two terms as senator. After he left office in 1979, it would be fourteen years before another African American would sit in the United States Senate.

The Black Panther Party was organized in California. It rejected the concept of integration, opting for separatism. With cries of "Black Power" and advocating for self-reliance, the organization became targets of police and the FBI. The group organized breakfast and lunch programs for inner-city school children.

Robert Weaver became the first African American to hold a cabinet position, serving as Secretary of Housing and Urban Development.

Five years after the United States started sending troops into Vietnam, African American troops constituted twenty percent of this country's

The United Methodist Church

1966 The World Division had been a predominantly white, male-oriented segment of the Board of Missions. That changed with the hiring of Grant Shockley and Rose Catchings. Dr. Shockley was hired first, but prior commitments kept him from arriving until after Ms. Catchings had been hired. Catchings's responsibility was to create and administer a program to aid women and children. Catchings was an intimidating force to white missionaries. She was well-educated and fluent in Malay and Spanish as well as English.

casualties. Charges were being made that African American troops were bearing the brunt of the war. The draft conscripted only 31 percent of eligible Whites but 64 percent of eligible African Americans. Over ninety-eight percent of draft officials were white.

1967
The United States had been involved in the Vietnam War for six years, and Dr. Martin Luther King, Jr., began to speak out more forcefully against it. Prior to that time, not many African Americans were involved in peace demonstrations that were taking place around the country.

Dr. King received a lot of criticism for speaking against the war. Many of the white "liberals" began to withdraw their support of and participation in the civil rights movement. Some civil rights organizations, including the NAACP, began to distance themselves from King, wanting to maintain separation between the peace movement and the civil rights movement. Some with political agendas or ties did not want to alienate themselves from white power structures. Yet the growing number of African American casualties was adding to the unrest in American cities.

Long hot summer was the term applied to the unrest of demonstrations, peace marches, and riots taking place. Temperatures in some areas rose to scorching levels, as did tempers. Riots erupted in neighborhoods in major cities across the country. President Lyndon Johnson created the National Advisory Commission in Civic Disorder, or the Kerner Commission, led by Illinois Governor Otto Kerner, to study the causes of the growing number

1967
L. Scott Allen was elected bishop in the last jurisdictional conference of the Central Jurisdiction.

of riots and to recommend solutions. The commission reported that 130 riots broke out during the summer of 1967.

President Lyndon Johnson appointed Thurgood Marshall to the Supreme Court, the first African American justice. Mr. Marshall had won twenty-nine of the thirty-two cases he argued before the Supreme Court.

Thurgood Marshall

1968
The Kerner Commission issued its report identifying a number of underlying causes of urban rioting and offering recommendations. One of the findings was that all the major incidents during that period were the result of arrests of African Americans for minor offenses or by other insensitive acts of white police in African American neighborhoods. *White terrorism* was a term used in one of the findings.

On April 4, Dr. Martin Luther King, Jr., was assassinated in Memphis, Tennessee. He had been in Memphis to give support to striking garbage collectors. Dr. King was struck down on the balcony of the Lorraine Motel. Riots erupted across the country as African Americans expressed anger and outrage.

1968
The United Methodist Church came into being through the Uniting Conference in Dallas, Texas, April 23, 1968. The church was a union between The Methodist Church and The Evangelical United Brethren Church. With this uniting, the Central Jurisdiction was abolished. It would, however, be five years before all of the Central Jurisdiction's annual conferences were merged into geographical jurisdictions. The union of the church did not come without vigorous dissent, particularly from Southerners who did not want the church integrated.

The Northeastern Jurisdiction elected Roy C. Nichols the first African American bishop in The United Methodist Church.

Two hundred fifty-nine registered delegates from every jurisdiction met in a National Conference of Negro Methodists in Cincinnati,

The World

At the Olympics in Mexico City two African Americans, Tommie Smith and John Carlos, gave the Black Power salute (raised fist) on the medals stand. They lost their medals because of this act.

Arthur Ashe won the men's title at the first U.S. Open tennis championship at Forest Hills, New York.

The King Center for Nonviolent Social Change was founded in Atlanta, Georgia, by Coretta Scott King, widow of Dr. Martin Luther King, Jr.

Shirley Chisholm, United Methodist laywoman from New York, was the first African American woman elected to Congress. In 1972 she was the first African American to run for President of the United States. Her political theme was "unbossed and unbought."

1969 James Earl Ray, a white ex-convict, was tried and sentenced to ninety-nine years in prison for the assassination of Dr. Martin Luther King, Jr. It is commonly believed that he could not have acted alone and then fled the country without accomplices, but none have been identified.

The United Methodist Church

Ohio. (Among the participants were James Farmer and Stokely Carmichael, who later chose their own methods for dealing with the issues of race.) Rev. James Lawson was elected Chairperson. A new organization called Black Methodists for Church Renewal (BMCR) resulted from the work of this conference.

Effective lobbying by African American Methodists, including Black Methodists for Church Renewal, led the General Conference to create the General Commission on Religion and Race. Dr. Woodie W. White, clergyman, became the first Executive Secretary, later General Secretary.

Miss Theressa Hoover became Associate General Secretary (chief executive officer) of the Women's Division of The United Methodist Board of Global Ministries. She held that position until her retirement in 1990.

Two other African American staff were hired. Minnie Stein of Austin, Texas, was chosen to serve as the Secretary of Legislative Affairs, and Cornelia Lake Smith of Baltimore became a regional staff person working out of Nashville, Tennessee.

1969 On December 13, 1969, in a special session of the Northern Illinois Conference, Chicago Black Methodists was adopted as a missional priority. This priority represented a change in the way ministry would be conducted in the conference. This conference was the first to adopt such a priority. Because the caucus was

The World

Police in several cities launched a crackdown against the Black Panther Party.

African American students took over buildings on the campus of Brandeis University. Their demands included a program in African American studies and better representation among staff and faculty. At Cornell, months later, students occupied a building to protest racist policies at the school. Similar acts took place on other campuses.

Harvard University instituted a program in Afro-American studies.

The Office of Minority Business Enterprise was created by presidential executive order.

The United Methodist Church

included in the budget of the Conference Council of Ministries, the group was able to open an office and offer a variety of services to the many struggling congregations as well as to help the conference remain faithful to the gospel with regard to the conference's African American constituency. In 1972 the caucus hired a young elder, William T. Carter, as Executive Director. During Carter's tenure the organization engaged in advocacy, mission, and services for congregations. Congregational Strong Centers emerged as a way to strengthen churches. A congregational economic committee was set up to provide small grants to churches for various mission projects. Later this caucus established the first, and for a while the only, ministerial recruitment and leadership development program for black youth and young adults. Out of this program emerged many elders and leaders in the Northern Illinois Conference.

African American staff at the General Board of Global Ministries formed their own Black Staff Network.

On May 4, James Forman, an African American 'militant,' strode into Riverside Church in New York, interrupting worship services and reading a "Black Manifesto." The manifesto was a call for reparations from white Christian churches, to be used for the economic development of African Americans.

THE DECADE OF THE 1970's

*A*ntiwar sentiments escalated on many college campuses. The killing of four Kent State students by the Ohio National Guard became a defining moment in America's history. Mandatory busing in some cities caused racial turmoil even in the northeast in places like Boston, the cradle of liberty. The Education for All Handicapped Children Act passed. Technology made an impact with the introduction of the floppy disc, the microprocessor, and the videocassette recorder. And the first test tube baby was born. Enrollment of women in college outnumbered enrollment of men; divorce rates soared; and women became more involved in politics. Affirmative Action became controversial although white women were more beneficiaries than ethnics. African Americans became more assertive and made their presence felt in Congress and in mayoral elections across the country. An American president resigned in disgrace.

1970
Results in congressional elections meant that thirteen African Americans would be seated in the 92nd Congress.

Antiwar demonstrations continued across the country on many college campuses. On May 4, during a demonstration at Kent State University in Ohio, four students were killed when national guardsmen opened fire. Nine others were shot and injured.

Dr. Clifton R. Wharton, Jr. became the first African American to head a major white institution of higher learning when he was elected president of Michigan State University. Dr. Wharton, an economist, had been the first African American to earn a Ph.D. in economics from the University of Chicago.

1970
A special session of the General Conference was convened in St. Louis as an adjourned session of the 1968 General Conference. Black Methodists for Church Renewal made a presentation on the needs for education and economic development. Several hundred African Americans quietly encircled the delegates sitting in the arena. The General Conference adopted some of the recommendations, authorizing

- an allocation for the General Commission on Religion and Race for administration of a Minority Group Economic Empowerment;
- a goal of $4 million a year in donations for support of twelve United Methodist black colleges;
- the General Board of Education to administer a $1 million scholarship fund for minority students.

The World

Charles Gordone won a Pulitzer Prize for his play *No Place to Be Somebody*. He was the first African American to win a Pulitzer for drama.

Doris Davis, a member of Wesley Methodist Church in Los Angeles, was elected mayor of Compton, California. She was the first African American woman elected as mayor of a metropolitan city. Doris grew up in Chicago in Hartzell Memorial Methodist Church.

1971 The African American members of the United States House of Representatives organized themselves as the Congressional Black Caucus to work for the interests of and in behalf of Black America.

Many school systems began using busing as a means of creating integrated schools.

African American writer Ernest J. Gaines's novel *The Autobiography of Miss Jane Pittman* was published. In 1974 it was made into a television movie that received high praise.

Johnson Products (cosmetics) was the first company owned by an African American to be listed on the American Stock Exchange.

The United Methodist Church

The General Commission on Religion and Race made a report to the General Conference of its findings, general observations, and recommendations regarding the status of the merged Central Jurisdiction conferences within the geographical jurisdictions. The report stated that organized opposition to the merger was occurring in Mississippi and Alabama. The report also noted that the women were already ahead of the general church, with Women's Societies already meeting together interracially.

For the first time, the General Conference had to adjourn because of a lack of a quorum due to the departure of many delegates.

1971 United Methodist Women was formed.

The National Black Methodists for Church Renewal (BMCR) and the Black Staff Forum met on November 20–21. A General Conference Task Force was created to consider issues that would be important to address for the 1972 General Conference, the first regular General Conference since the merger of the Central Jurisdiction into the geographical jurisdictions. Significant issues emerged in the areas of social consciousness and investments; structure study reports; and *Discipline* revisions in the areas of the Social Creed, ministerial qualifications, and employment practices. C. Leonard Miller was the chairperson of the group that later met in Atlanta.

The World

People United to Save Humanity (PUSH) was organized in Chicago by Jesse Jackson, African American civil rights activist and minister.

1972 The United States government revealed its forty-year involvement in the Tuskegee Syphilis Experiment.

The U.S. Congress passed the Equal Employment Opportunity Act.

On May 17 an African American guard discovered agents of the Republican Party in the process of burglarizing the Democratic National Committee headquarters at the Watergate Hotel in Washington, DC. This action was later traced back to the White House and led to the resignation of President Nixon.

Barbara Jordan, from Houston, Texas, was elected to the United States House of Representatives and became a member of the Judiciary Committee. Jordan had been the first woman elected to the Texas State Senate and was the first southern African American woman elected to the United States Congress. She distinguished herself with her eloquence during the Watergate Investigation.

1973 On January 22 the Supreme Court decision in *Roe* v. *Wade* legalized abortion.

On October 10 Spiro Agnew, Vice President of the United States, was forced to resign amid charges of corruption and tax evasion.

The United Methodist Church

MARCHA, the Hispanic/Latino caucus of the church, was organized.

1972 The 1972 General Conference was the first one following the historic church union and the realignment of some of the Central Jurisdiction conferences. It was the first General Conference of The United Methodist Church.

The General Conference created the Commission on the Status and Role of Women. Barbara Ricks Thompson was the first president.

The General Conference took action to restructure the general agencies of the church. It created the General Board of Discipleship, forged from several boards and commissions.

Ernest T. Dixon, Jr., was elected to the episcopacy in the South Central Jurisdiction, and Edward G. Carroll was elected in the Northeastern Jurisdiction.

The black South Carolina Conference merged with the South Carolina Annual Conference.

1973 Rev. Dr. Melvin G. Talbert (an African American district superintendent from Long Beach, California) was elected as the first General Secretary of the General Board of Discipleship (GBOD). Not only did he have the task of uniting the independent units of the GBOD into one cohesive body, but the newly elected

The World

On December 6 Michigan congressman Gerald Ford was sworn in as the new Vice President of the United States. The following August he was sworn in as President when Richard Nixon resigned. Nixon was facing impeachment proceedings because of involvement in Watergate.

African Americans awakened to newfound political power. Among African Americans elected mayor of major cities were Thomas Bradley in Los Angeles, Maynard Jackson in Atlanta, and Coleman Young in Detroit.

Illinois was the first state to designate the birthday of Dr. Martin Luther King, Jr., a holiday.

African American lawyer and social justice activist Marian Wright Edelman founded the Children's Defense Fund, an organization focused on advancing the interests of children and poor families.

The United Methodist Church

executive had the challenges of racism as well. When he came to that office, former heads of boards and commissions who were now his associates did not want to relinquish power, offices, or budgets. He was offered a "big and convenient office" in the basement. However, a number of justice-minded people prevailed in the fight among board members and staff, and Talbert was given the executive office on the second floor. In assessing the operations of all the units, Talbert discovered that the newly created agency was facing a severe financial deficit. Frank conversations with board members provided a means for Talbert to gain needed control of finances. The GBOD operated without deficits during the remainder of his tenure.

African American members of the board of directors of the GBOD included David L. White, a layman from Jeffersonville, Indiana; Allen Brown, a layman from New Orleans, Louisiana; Bishop Edward G. Carroll, Boston Area; Bishop James S. Thomas, Iowa Area; and Rev. Henry C. Clay from Mississippi.

The General Board of Discipleship sponsored a Consultation on the Black Church in Atlanta, Georgia. Out of the consultation came the National Advisory Task Force to develop a worship resource, resulting in *Songs of Zion*. Published by Abingdon Press in 1981, this supplemental worship resource contains hymns, spirituals, and gospel songs out of the experiences of African Americans. The book was edited by J. Jefferson Cleveland and Verolga Nix. Dr. William B. McClain was the chairperson of the task force. Other African Americans serving on the task force with Dr. McClain and Dr. Talbert, the General Secretary of the Board, were Fletcher J. Bryant, Cynthia Felder, Douglass Fitch, Zan Holmes, Charlotte Meade, Maceo Pembroke, Israel Rucker, Forrest C. Stith, and Ethelou Talbert.

The Northern Illinois Chapter of Black Methodists for Church Renewal hosted its first Ministerial Recruitment and Leadership Development Program. Conceptualized by Dr. Philip A. Harley, the concept was to engage youth in a one-week retreat of learning, exposing them to the best of clergy and laypeople in a variety of professions and creating an environment in which they would see ministry as a viable vocational option. The program was named The Pembroke Institute after the Rev. Dr. Maceo D. Pembroke, who died while in retreat with the young people in 1981.

The final merger of all Central Jurisdiction congregations into the geographical jurisdictions took place in this year. Mississippi was the last state to complete the mergers.

One of the issues confronted by the new General Commission on Religion and Race was that some annual conferences were trying to practice dualism in appointments of district superintendents; that is, African American district superintendents supervised black churches while white district superintendents supervised white churches.

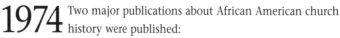

The World

1974 Federal District Court Judge Arthur Garrity ruled that the school board in Boston, Massachusetts, was deliberately maintaining segregation and that schools there must be integrated. Whites rioted in an attempt to block a court-ordered school-integration busing plan. Schools and streets became battlegrounds. Rifle fire was directed into the *Boston Globe* newspaper offices.

In the judiciary hearings determining impeachment charges against President Richard Nixon, African American congresswoman Barbara Jordan captivated listeners with her speech acknowledging that "we the people" in the Constitution originally did not include her but that she wholly believed in the Constitution.

African American singer/songwriter Stevie Wonder's album *Innervisions* won the Grammy Award for album of the year.

African American Henry (Hank) Aaron established a new baseball record for career homeruns.

The economy was in the worst recession in forty years.

1975 Frank Robinson became manager of the Cleveland Indians. He was the first African American manager of a major-league baseball team.

The United Methodist Church

1974 Two major publications about African American church history were published:

- *Dark Salvation: The Story of Methodism As It Developed Among Blacks in America*, by Dr. Harry V. Richardson, published by Doubleday. Dr. Richardson had served as president of Gammon Theological Seminary (1948–1959), president of Interdenominational Theological Seminary, chaplain at Tuskegee in Alabama, and executive secretary and field director for rural ministry. He received his Ph.D. from Drew University.
- Dr. James P. Brawley's significant reference, *Two Centuries of Methodist Concern: Bondage, Freedom, and Education of Black People*. Dr. Brawley was one of Methodism's most respected scholars and educators.

The National Federation of Asian-American United Methodists was formed.

The World

Daniel "Chappie" James was promoted to four-star general in the U.S. Air Force. He was the first African American to attain this rank.

Harvard University founded the W.E.B. DuBois Institute for Afro-American Research, named for the first African American to receive a Ph.D. from Harvard (in 1895).

Lee Elder became the first African American golfer to play in the Masters Tournament.

1976 Congresswoman Barbara Jordan became the first African American to deliver a keynote address at a national convention of the Democratic Party.

Congressional investigation reports and FBI documents revealed a major effort by the FBI, through its COINTELPRO activities, to discredit and undermine the civil rights movement in the 1960's.

Alex Haley's book *Roots* was published, offering a reconstruction of the African American author's family history as they journeyed from an African village to slavery in America. It became a national bestseller and the winner of a special Pulitzer Prize. The book and subsequent television miniseries sparked many Americans to explore family genealogy and many African American families to hold reunions.

The United Methodist Church

1976 The missional priority "to strengthen the ethnic minority church" was established at the General Conference.

Bishop Edsel Albert Ammons was the first African American bishop elected in the North Central Jurisdiction. Bishop Ammons, from the Northern Illinois Conference, was serving as Professor of Urban Ministries at Garrett Theological Seminary at the time of his election. He had pastored congregations and had served on conference staff prior to going to Garrett. He was the second African American to serve on the seminary staff.

George Outen became General Secretary for the General Board of Church and Society, holding the position until his untimely death in 1980, when he suffered a massive heart attack on Christmas Eve.

Mai H. Gray became the first African American woman to serve as president of the Women's Division. In the same year, Adelaide V.

The World

1977 African Americans were making strides in national political recognition; but for the masses, racism continued to be manifested in education, employment, law enforcement, justice, and social arenas.

Clifford Alexander was appointed as Secretary of the Army. He was the first African American to hold this post.

Patricia Roberts Harris was appointed as Secretary of Housing and Urban Development. She was the first African American woman to serve on the cabinet of a President.

Andrew Young was appointed as U.S. ambassador to the United Nations. He was the first African American to hold this position.

The TV miniseries *Roots*, based on Alex Haley's book, set records for viewership across the country, sparking much discussion in schools and places of employment. The series was acknowledged with a number of Emmy Awards.

A member of the Ku Klux Klan was the first man convicted in the 1963 bombing of Birmingham's Sixteenth Street Baptist Church.

The United Methodist Church

Barnes of Washington, DC, was elected recording secretary.

Dorothy Height, an active United Methodist, followed Dr. Mary McLeod Bethune as President of the National Council of Negro Women.

1977 Dr. Joseph Lowery became head of the Southern Christian Leadership Council. Dr. Lowery has had a distinguished career in the pastoral ministries and civil rights.

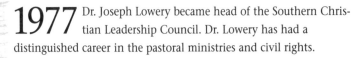

The World

1978 In a court action brought by Allan Bakke charging "reverse discrimination" against the University of California, the Supreme Court struck down the policy of the University to reserve spaces in its medical school for minorities. This would be the forerunner to the erosion of affirmative action.

Max Robinson became the first African American news anchor on a network when he anchored ABC's *World News Tonight*.

1979 The miniseries *Roots: The Next Generations*, sequel to the 1977 miniseries *Roots*, aired on network television (ABC).

Rap music emerged as a form of popular music, appealing to a young audience. Rap's anti-establishment lyrics drew much criticism from both African Americans and Whites.

The United Methodist Church

1979 Rev. John H. Graham, a staff member of the General Board of Global Ministries, published *Black United Methodists: Retrospect and Prospect*, a short history of Methodism among black Americans since 1738.

THE DECADE OF THE 1980'S

The eighties became the spending years, or the decade of decadence, as shopping, status, and credit became the rage among those who could afford it and those who could not. Credit debt soared. In the business world it was open season on buyouts, takeovers, and megamergers. The rich and famous became household conversations. Computers became more affordable, and large numbers of people began to use them in their homes. Issues of poverty, illiteracy, and poor schooling were still with us, but in many instances they were pushed onto the backburners of government and political leaders.

Sad days in the nation included watching the space shuttle Challenger explode shortly after takeoff. Wayne Williams was arrested in connection with the murder of twenty-nine African-American children and young adults, and AIDS began to emerge as a rabid killer. The number of one-parent families grew rapidly. Violent crime rates rose with the appearance of a potent drug, crack. Like no other kind of drug, this one seemed to take away the humanity of its users.

Appointments to the Supreme Court during the 1980's and 1990's changed the way the Court viewed discrimination. Rulings by the Court made it more difficult for individual and class-action lawsuits charging job discrimination to be filed.

African American writers Toni Morrison and Alice Walker were two of the most-read authors of the decade.

1980 Ronald Reagan was elected President of the United States.

Riots erupted in Miami after white policemen were acquitted in the beating death of an African American.

Dr. John B. Slaughter, electrical engineer, became the first African American director of the National Science Foundation.

1980 The General Conference convened in Indianapolis, Indiana. There was increased visibility of African Americans in delegations and in leadership.

Native Americans made their presence known at the General Conference by establishing a tent outside the convention center.

In the jurisdictional elections, history was made when Marjorie Matthews, a white woman from the North Central Jurisdiction, became the first woman elected bishop. She was assigned to the Wisconsin Area, where she served one quadrennium.

Three African Americans were elected bishop: Bishop William T. Handy, Jr., in the South Central Jurisdiction; Bishop F. Herbert Skeet in the Northeastern Jurisdiction; and Bishop Melvin G. Talbert, the first African American to be elected in the Western Jurisdiction.

Bishop Edsel Ammons, African American bishop from the North Central Jurisdiction, was elected president of the General Board of Discipleship. He had served on the board of directors since 1976.

Bishop James S. Thomas was the first African American president of the General Council on Finance and Administration.

1981 An assassination attempt was made on President Ronald Reagan.

Labor unions and civil rights groups staged a march in Washington, DC, that included more than 300,000 people. They marched to protest President Reagan's policies opposed to unions, affirmative action, and social programs.

1982 The Voting Rights Act of 1965 was extended for another twenty-five years. The extension of the voting rights was vigorously opposed by the Reagan administration. Although there were setbacks in court decisions, the Act did reenfranchise and empower African Americans, resulting not only in an increase in registered voters but also in an increase in the number of political office holders.

1982 Dr. Randolph Nugent, an African American from the New York Conference, became the General Secretary of the General Board of Global Ministries after serving as the head of the Board's National Division for a number of years. In addition to his many credentials, Dr. Nugent was proficient in several languages.

The World

Hank Aaron was inducted into the Baseball Hall of Fame. Aaron was the last Negro League player to also play in the major leagues.

1983 The third Monday of January was designated as an annual federal holiday in observance of the January 15 birthday of Dr. Martin Luther King, Jr. This was the first federally designated holiday recognizing the birthday of an African American.

The city of Chicago, Illinois, elected its first African American mayor, Harold Washington. His administration was one of the most diverse in the history of Chicago politics. He was reelected in 1987 but died of a heart attack soon after.

The Color Purple, a novel by African American writer Alice Walker about the life and trials of a young African American woman, won the Pulitzer Prize for fiction. It was later made into a movie starring Whoopi Goldberg and featuring Danny Glover and Oprah Winfrey among others.

Colonel Guion S. Bluford, Jr., orbited the earth aboard the space shuttle Challenger. He was the first African American in space.

1984 Jesse Jackson ran for the Democratic presidential nomination. African Americans responded with unprecedented support in the form of volunteerism, registration, and contributions to a political campaign.

The United Methodist Church

Leontyne T. C. Kelly. See 1984 on page 126.

1984 This year marked the two hundredth anniversary of Methodism. The General Conference met in Baltimore, Maryland. Developing and strengthening the ethnic local church continued as the missional priority of the church.

The World

DeLores Tucker founded the National Political Caucus of Black Women. Shirley Chisholm was elected as the first chairperson.

The Cosby Show began airing on NBC, starring African American comedian Bill Cosby and a host of characters who became America's favorite family. While the series earned critical acclaim and top ratings, it taught Americans about relationships, alternative means for child rearing, the significance of grandparents, Black art, historically Black colleges, and other aspects of Black culture. All of the actors portraying the children in the show went on to further acting or directing roles, and some pursued other important interests as well.

African American athlete Carl Lewis won four gold medals in track-and-field events at the Olympic Games in Los Angeles.

1985 Stevie Wonder, Michael Jackson, and other musical artists recorded the song and video "We Are the World," produced to raise funds to fight famine in Africa. The record became a major success. The effort was led by African American musical arranger, composer, and industry executive Quincy Jones.

Gwendolyn Brooks became poet laureate of the United States.

1986 Oprah Winfrey's talk show premiered nationally on television, making her the first female African American host of a nationwide talk show.

The United Methodist Church

Leontyne T. C. Kelly from the Southeast Jurisdiction was elected bishop in the Western Jurisdiction, making her the first African American woman elected bishop in any mainline denomination. At the time of her election, Bishop Kelly was an Assistant General Secretary in Evangelism at the General Board of Discipleship. Her election was the result of an intentional campaign led by a women's movement and a coalition of ethnic people and others.

Other African Americans elected to the episcopacy were Bishop Felton Edwin May in the Northeastern Jurisdiction; Bishop Ernest Newman, the first African American to be elected in the Southeastern Jurisdiction; Bishop Forrest C. Stith in the Northeastern Jurisdiction; and Bishop Woodie W. White in the North Central Jurisdiction.

1985 Barbara Ricks Thompson, laywoman, became General Secretary of the General Commission on Religion and Race, the second person to lead that commission.

Harold Batiste, an African American from the Southwest Texas Conference, became president of the National Association of Annual Conference Presidents of United Methodist Men. He was elected for a second term in 1987.

1986 Marilyn W. Magee became the Assistant General Secretary for Ministry of the Laity at the General Board of Discipleship. In January she had been featured in *Essence* magazine in an article about black women and spirituality. Magee and David L. White were the only African American heads of program ministries at the General Board of Discipleship.

1987 In January, Clarence "Du" Burns became Baltimore's first African American mayor when he was appointed to finish the incomplete term of office left by the previous mayor. In November, Kurt Schmoke was elected mayor, becoming the first African American elected to the office.

Johnnetta Cole became Spelman College's first African American female president.

Reginald Lewis bought out Beatrice International Foods and formed TLC Beatrice, which became the largest company in the United States owned by an African American.

1987 Ernest Swiggett, a layman from the New York Annual Conference, became the first African American treasurer of any United Methodist annual conference. He later served as president of National Black Methodists for Church Renewal (BMCR). His election as a delegate to the 2004 General Conference marked the fifth time he had served in that capacity.

1988 Jesse Jackson tried a second time to gain the Democratic nomination for President, rallying African American voters again and winning the second largest number of delegates.

An estimated 60,000 people participated in a new March on Washington on the twenty-fifth anniversary of the 1963 march.

Spelman College announced a $20 million gift from Bill and Camille Cosby.

1988 The General Conference convened in St. Louis, Missouri. Dr. John G. Corry, a distinguished scholar, pastor, professor, and activist, was elected to the Judicial Council.

Joseph B. Bethea was elected bishop in the Southeastern Jurisdiction.

Two jurisdictions now had three African American bishops: Thomas (1964), Ammons (1976), and White (1984) in the North Central

The World

At the Olympic Games in Seoul, African American athletes Florence Griffith-Joyner, Jackie Joyner-Kersee, and Carl Lewis dominated the competition in track-and-field events.

The United Methodist Church

Jurisdiction; Skeete (1980), May (1984), and Stith (1984) in the Northeastern Jurisdiction.

Bishop James S. Thomas, who had previously chaired the General Commission on Finance and Administration (GCFA), became the first African American bishop to chair the General Council on Ministries (GCOM).

Bishop Melvin G. Talbert was the first African American elected secretary of the Council of Bishops.

National Black Methodists for Church Renewal (BMCR) celebrated its twentieth anniversary in Oakland, California. Marilyn W. Magee, laywoman and vice chairperson, presided. Special tribute was made to Dr. Negail Riley, whose doctoral thesis examined the foundation for the establishment of the Community Developers program at the General Board of Global Ministries. A scholarship was initiated in his name.

One of BMCR's major undertakings was the Black Church Growth Consultation, "Black Pentecost," held August 25–28 in Atlanta, Georgia. Members of the design team and work group included Bishops Woodie W. White, Forrest C. Stith, and Roy C. Nichols; Dr. James Shropshire, Wesley Theological Seminary; Dr Alfred Norris, President of Gammon Seminary; Dr. Warren Hill, Staff, General Commission on Religion and Race; William T. Robinson, Staff, General Board of Global Ministries; C. Leonard Miller, Staff, General Council on Ministries; Mary Hicks Good, Staff, General Board of Global Ministries; David White, Staff, General Board of Discipleship; John G. Corry,

The World

1989 African American priest Barbara Harris was consecrated as a bishop in the Episcopal Church. She was the first female bishop in the Anglican communion.

General Colin L. Powell was appointed Chairman of the Joint Chiefs of Staff. He was the first African American to hold this position.

Voters in New York City elected David Dinkins as mayor. He was the city's first African American mayor.

L. Douglas Wilder was elected governor of Virginia. He was the first African American in the nation to be elected governor.

The film *Glory*, with Denzel Washington and Morgan Freeman, portrayed the actions of the 54th Regiment of Massachusetts during the Civil War.

Bill White became president of baseball's National League, the first league president who was an African American.

Of U.S. households with televisions, nearly sixty percent had cable.

The United Methodist Church

chairperson of National BMCR; Marilyn W. Magee, vice chairperson of BMCR; Carolyn Anderson, Executive Director of BMCR; and Deborah Bass, consultant. Teams of congregations came from across the connection for intensive training.

THE DECADE OF THE 1990's

1990 In February, Nelson Mandela, a leader in the struggle against apartheid in South Africa, was released after twenty-seven years in prison. Shortly thereafter, Mr. Mandela toured major U.S. cities and delivered an address to Congress.

The Middle Passage, by African American writer and cartoonist Charles Johnson, won the National Book Award for fiction.

African American actor Denzel Washington won an Academy Award for Best Supporting Actor for his role in *Glory*.

The Americans With Disabilities Act was signed into law in July, changing the way the rights of all people, regardless of disabilities, are respected. Most of the act's rules went into effect in 1992.

1991 U.S. Supreme Court Justice Thurgood Marshall retired. He had served since appointment by President Johnson in 1967.

1990 Nelson Mandela appeared in Atlanta, Georgia, shortly after being released from prison. This was the first place he had appeared in the United States since his release. Marilyn W. Magee, Assistant General Secretary for Christian Education and Laity at the General Board of Discipleship, and Angella Current, Associate General Secretary of the General Board of Higher Education and Ministry, drove to Atlanta for the appearance. They were the guests of Angella's cousin, Aaron Turpeau, who was the mayor's Chief of Staff (and member of Cascade United Methodist Church). The two staff members watched with excitement from the "up-front crowd" as Mr. Mandela's plane landed. Later they attended a luncheon for Winnie Mandela facilitated by Maya Angelou.

Bishop Felton E. May was granted authorization by the Council of Bishops to lead the church in addressing the issues of alcohol and other drug abuse. African American lay staff from the denomination's boards and agencies collaborated with staffs of the African Methodist Episcopal (AME), African Methodist Episcopal Zion (AMEZ), and Christian Methodist Episcopal (CME) communions to develop curriculum resources and training for congregational leaders to fight abuse of drugs.

The World

African American Clarence Thomas was nominated to fill the Supreme Court vacancy left by Thurgood Marshall's retirement. He was confirmed even though civil rights groups opposed his appointment and Anita Hill charged that Thomas had sexually harassed her when she worked for him years earlier.

Almost twenty-five percent of the U.S. troops in service in Operation Desert Storm were African Americans.

Los Angeles police officers were caught on videotape beating Rodney King, an African American motorist the police had stopped for allegedly speeding. The videotape was broadcast nationwide, sparking outrage across the country.

Dr. Walter Massey, physicist, became the second African American director of the National Science Foundation. Dr. Massey earned his Ph.D. at Washington University in St. Louis, Missouri.

1992
The World Wide Web was released for use. The Web would go on to change our methods of communicating, shopping, doing business, conducting research, and searching for information of all kinds. Technology sped up everything and introduced a new vocabulary.

Four white policemen were acquitted of beating African American motorist Rodney King in Los Angeles. Upon publicity of the verdict, a fifty-square-mile area in Los Angeles erupted in violent rioting, resulting in the

The United Methodist Church

1992
The General Conference met in Louisville, Kentucky.

The first African American clergywomen were appointed to the district superintendency: Rev. J. Jeannette Cooper, West Ohio Conference, North Central Jurisdiction, was appointed effective June 15 by Bishop Edsel Ammons. Rev. Mary Brown Oliver, Baltimore Conference, Northeastern Jurisdiction, was appointed effective July 1. Rev. Charlotte death of over fifty people and an estimated one billion dollars of damage to property and businesses. President George Bush called out 4,500 troops to quell the disturbances. In August, following further investigation by the Criminal Section and the U.S. Attorney's Office in Los Angeles, the four officers were indicted for the beating. A federal trial ended in the conviction of two of the officers.

The Nobel Prize for Literature went to Derek Walcott, a poet from St. Lucia, making him the first black winner of the prize from the Western Hemisphere.

Carol Moseley-Braun was the first African American female senator. Elected from Illinois, Braun was educated in Chicago schools and graduated from the University of Chicago School of Law. She was defeated after serving one term.

In September, Mae Jemison, the first African American woman to be admitted into the astronaut training program, also became the first to fly in space. Her eight-day space mission was successful.

Nichols, Peninsula Conference, Northeastern Jurisdiction, was appointed effective July 1. These were historic appointments, especially after so many years of service by African American women in ordained ministry.

Elected to the episcopacy were Charles Wesley Jordan, North Central Jurisdiction; William Wesley Morris, Southeastern Jurisdiction; and Alfred Norris, South Central Jurisdiction.

Dr. Carolyn E. Johnson became president of the Women's Division of the United Methodist Board of Global Ministries, the second African American woman to do so. Mrs. Mai Gray was the first.

The World

President-Elect William Jefferson Clinton appointed four African Americans to his cabinet: Ronald Brown, Hazel O'Leary, Jesse Brown, and Mike Espy.

1993

At the U.S. presidential inauguration of Bill Clinton, distinguished African American author, poet, and civil rights activist Maya Angelou read an original poem written for the occasion.

African American poet, playwright, and composer Rita Dove was appointed U.S. Poet Laureate.

Toni Morrison was awarded the Nobel Prize for Literature. No African American and no black woman, from any country, had won this prize before. She was recognized for six novels: *The Bluest Eye*, *Sula*, *Tar Baby*, *Song of Solomon*, *Beloved* (which won the Pulitzer Prize for Fiction in 1988), and *Jazz*.

Dr. Joycelyn Elders, a United Methodist laywoman from Arkansas, was confirmed as Surgeon General of the United States, the first African American to hold the position. She was later forced to resign because of her outspoken views on sexuality education. Dr. Elders returned to the University of Arkansas Medical Center as a professor.

The United Methodist Church

1993

Rev. Tallulah F. Williams, the first African American woman ordained in the Northern Illinois Conference following merger, became the first clergywoman elected to head National Black Methodists for Church Renewal (BMCR) at its twenty-fifth anniversary meeting in Cincinnati, Ohio. Rev. Williams was also the first African American female district superintendent in the Northern Illinois Conference. She died in Chicago, Illinois, a few days after being elected on the first ballot as the first delegate to the 2000 General Conference. She left a legacy of setting the mark for excellence. After serving as student pastor at St. Mark United Methodist Church, she served pastorates at Vincent United Methodist Church and Southlawn United Methodist Church. She became the first female pastor of Hartzell Memorial United Methodist Church prior to pastoring an all-white congregation in one of Chicago's suburbs. Tallulah's travels took her on many preaching engagements, including to Tonga. She and Marilyn W. Magee, author of this book and Executive Secretary for Family Ministries and Conference Relations at the General Board of Discipleship, developed a strong friendship when they shared a mission trip to Niger, West Africa, in 1982. They also shared a hobby of collecting black Madonna and Child figurines, often exchanging items obtained from their diverse travels.

1994
The November elections resulted in African Americans holding 41 seats in Congress but losing the chair positions of three committees as the Republicans controlled Congress for the first time in several years.

By the end of the year, an estimated ten million people were using the World Wide Web.

1995
On April 19 the nation was shocked by the bombing of the Federal Building in Oklahoma City. Initially there were fears that the act had been committed by terrorists. The next shock was that the act had been committed by a United States Army veteran, Timothy McVeigh.

Shirley Ann Jackson, physicist, became the first African American to chair the Nuclear Regulatory Commission. In 1973 she had been the first African American woman to receive a Ph.D. from the Massachusetts Institute of Technology.

More than one million African American men came together in Washington, DC, for the Million Man March to draw attention to the social problems of African Americans. Some people had concerns because the March grew out the Nation of Islam's call for a day of reflection and atonement, but in the end the rally drew more African Americans than the 1963 March on Washington. While the march was a rallying cry for

The World

African American men to assume control of their lives, some women also went, and women were included among the speakers. Speaker after speaker addressed the strengths of African American men and of the systems in place that contributed to negative images. The men were admonished to step forward and assume responsibility for their children and others as well. In spite of dire predictions and a strong presence of law enforcement, the march was peaceful.

1996 Voters in the State of California approved Proposition 209, which forbade the use of any form of affirmative action policies in state governments, local governments, districts, public universities, colleges, and schools. Many feared that this action would lead to a nationwide trend. However, several state legislatures have voted down or refused to act on bills modeled after the California bill.

In the largest discrimination case in U.S. history, Texaco settled, agreeing to pay $176 million to 1,400 current and former African American employees.

Kweisi Mfume, an African American member of the U.S. House of Representatives and former leader of the Congressional Black Caucus, was chosen to head the NAACP. Mfume rose from humble circumstances to succeed the legendary politician Parren J. Mitchell in the United States Congress. As head of the NAACP he eradicated its excessive debt and revitalized the organization and its appeal to young African Americans.

The United Methodist Church

1996 The General Conference meeting in Denver, Colorado, passed legislation authorizing "Strengthening the Black Church for the 21st Century" as a mission initiative. The initiative's goal was to develop a model for enabling vital congregations to help revitalize other congregations. The goals were realized as the Coordinating Committee made plans to establish twenty-five Congregation Resource Centers for training lay and clergy teams to serve as mentors for other congregations. The objective was to develop ministry models that would fit varying geographic and special needs with a strong focus on the gifts and skills of laypeople.

Four new African American bishops were elected: Alfred Johnson and Ernest S. Lyght in the Northeastern Jurisdiction; Jonathan D. Keaton in the North Central Jurisdiction; and Cornelius L. Henderson in the Southeastern Jurisdiction.

The World

Secretary of Commerce Ron Brown, one of four African Americans serving in the cabinet of the Clinton administration, died in a plane crash during a humanitarian mission to Croatia. Ron Brown was the first African American to chair a national political party (Democrat) and the first African American chief counsel of a United States Senate standing committee.

1997 In a ceremony at the White House on May 16, President Clinton made a formal apology for exploitation of black patients during the Tuskegee syphilis experiment. The President acknowledged that the study and the government's role in it was "racist" and "profoundly, morally wrong." Five of the eight surviving men attended the special ceremony.

A Congressional Medal of Honor was belatedly awarded to seven African Americans for heroism during World War II.

The Million Woman March took place in Philadelphia. While it did not draw as many participants as the men's march and was mired in controversy, the organizers considered it a success because it happened at all.

The Virginia Senate voted to designate "Carry Me Back to Ol' Virginny" as state song emeritus and search for a new state song.

James Earl Ray, who was convicted of the 1968 assassination of Dr. Martin Luther King, Jr., died in prison.

The United Methodist Church

1997 The Coordinating Committee of Strengthening the Black Church for the 21st Century established the criteria and selection process for identifying Congregation Resource Centers (teaching congregations willing to share helpful resources, ideas, and so forth with Partner Congregations). Twenty-five congregations were named, inclusive of all jurisdictions, urban and rural settings, large and small memberships, and particular foci for congregational development.

Saint Mark United Methodist Church in Wichita, Kansas, was the first Congregation Resource Center to host a training session. This church, under the leadership of Rev. Tyrone Gordon, has become one of the fastest growing churches in the country. Participants in the Evangelism and Church Growth Institute discovered the meaning of hospitality and excellence in an effective learning conference.

The World

1998 The President's Commission on Race initiated national exploration of issues affecting African Americans. The commission was led by John Hope Franklin, distinguished African American historian and author.

Julian Bond, African American civil rights activist, veteran of the Georgia General Assembly, professor, and writer, was elected chair of the NAACP's board of directors.

According to government statistics, AIDS was taking a disproportionately heavier toll on African Americans than on other ethnic groups.

The *Pittsburgh Courier* won a special Polk Award as the top source of news geared to African American readers.

African American professional basketball player Michael Jordan led the Chicago Bulls to their sixth NBA championship in eight years.

More than 100 million people were using the World Wide Web.

1999 President Bill Clinton pardoned Henry O. Flipper, who in 1877 was the first African American graduate of West Point. Flipper had been shunned by fellow classmates during his entire time at West Point. No one spoke directly to him. He ate alone and spent his time isolated from any camaraderie. Flipper distinguished himself by leading the Buffalo Soldiers. Railroaded by the Army for a crime he did not commit, he

The United Methodist Church

1998 Barbara Ricks Thompson retired as General Secretary of the General Commission on Religion and Race. She was only the second person—the first woman and the first layperson—to hold the position since its creation in 1972. She was a former president of the Commission on the Status and Role of Women (1972–1978). Thompson has been an active leader in her local church. Currently she is co-chairing a new venture, an African American Methodist heritage center that will be housed in Atlanta, Georgia.

The David White Laity Award was established by National Black Methodists for Church Renewal (BMCR) at its meeting in Oakland, California. The first medallion was presented to Dr. David L. White, a layman from Jeffersonville, Indiana. He has been an active member of The United Methodist Church for many years, serving in various capacities in his local church, conference, and the general church. He has been active in North Central Jurisdiction BMCR and National BMCR. For several years, he served as the head of Ethnic Local Church Resourcing at the General Board of Discipleship. He retired in December 1996.

was dishonorably discharged in 1882. In 1976 Flipper was exonerated of wrongdoing and reburied with full honors. The pardoning speech, twenty-three years later, declared that it was time for the error to be corrected.

On April 20 the nation was shocked by school shootings at Columbine High School in Littleton, Colorado. Fourteen students, one of whom was African American, and one teacher were killed. Twenty-three others were wounded. The shooting was done by fellow students.

Although the twenty-first century did not actually begin until January 2001, the world prepared for the coming of a new millennium at the end of 1999. The decade of the 1990's ended amidst apprehension about the Y2K syndrome. Concerns about computers, which controlled so many facets of our lives, were rampant. Directions about preparing for the new millennium ranged from preserving food stuffs and stocking water to manuals for surviving for days without electricity.

In contrast to the survival mentality was the mass of celebrative events planned for New Year's Eve.

THE END OF THE TWENTIETH CENTURY: THE YEAR 2000

2000 For the first time, Martin Luther King, Jr., Day was celebrated in all fifty states. All but New Hampshire had celebrated the day by 1993, but New Hampshire did not approve a statewide King holiday until 1999, to be celebrated first in 2000.

2000 The General Conference convened in Cleveland, Ohio. Strengthening the Black Church for the 21st Century was renewed as a mission initiative. Among other actions taken by this General Conference was a change in the way the number of delegates from each conference would be calculated. This, in effect, reduced the number of delegates from the conferences in the Western Jurisdiction.

At the jurisdictional conferences, African American bishops were elected in each of the five jurisdictions. For the first time, seven African American bishops were elected in a single jurisdictional election period. They were Rhymes H. Moncure, Jr., South Central Jurisdiction; Beverly J. Shamana and Warner Brown, Western Jurisdiction; Violet L. Fisher, Northeastern Jurisdiction; Gregory V. Palmer and Linda Dobbins Lee, North Central Jurisdiction; and James R. King, Southeastern Jurisdiction. Beverly Shamana became the first African American woman elected to the episcopacy since the election of Bishop Leontyne Kelly in 1984.

In May, Rev. Dr. Atty. John G. Corry from Nashville, Tennessee, was elected president of the Judicial Council, the first African American clergy to hold the position. Corry was also named Chancellor of the Tennessee Conference in June. Dr. Corry had served the church with distinction in various other roles: pastor, district superintendent, chaplain at Meharry Medical College, national chairperson for Black Methodists for Church Renewal, and adviser and mentor to countless groups and individuals.

THE DAWN OF THE TWENTY-FIRST CENTURY

2001

In 1998 DNA had revealed the possibility of a direct ancestry relationship between Thomas Jefferson and the son of one of Jefferson's slaves, Sally Hemings. In 2001 the Hemings family was invited to the annual family gathering of Jefferson descendants on the grounds of Monticello. They were warmly welcomed at first but were later denied even honorary membership in the Monticello Association.

In May, Thomas Blanton, Jr., was convicted in the 1963 bombing of Sixteenth Street Baptist Church in Birmingham, Alabama.

On September 11, terrorists commandeered four airplanes and executed a widespread rein of unprecedented terror in the United States. American Airlines and United Airlines each lost two planes that were hijacked and used as missiles to strike the World Trade Center Twin Towers in New York City and the Pentagon building outside Washington, DC. Another plane missed its potential target, most likely the White House, due to the heroic actions of some of the passengers. The plane crashed in a field in Pennsylvania, killing all on board.

For several days all air flights were grounded, stranding thousands of people in and out of the country. Thousands of people lost their lives. Businesses and homes were destroyed and people were displaced. Stories of heroism and random acts of kindness abounded. Thousands of police,

2001

The Coordinating Committee of Strengthening the Black Church for the 21st Century met in Los Angeles. They had concluded their meeting and were preparing to leave on the morning of September 11 when terrorists attacked the World Trade Center in New York and the Pentagon in Washington, DC. Two members had left the hotel. Roderick McLean, staff member from the General Board of Global Ministries, was aboard an airborne plane that was forced to return to the airport. Ronald Coleman from the General Board of Pensions and Health Benefits was aboard a flight almost ready for departure when the passengers were told to deplane and leave the airport. Others were in various stages of departure. Fortunately, the hotel permitted committee members to stay at the same rate they had been given for the meeting. The group was stranded until flights resumed days later.

Some members of the committee were pulled into counseling sessions because the hotel in which the committee was staying became the gathering place for families of those aboard one of the airplanes bound for Los Angeles.

Bishop Jonathan D. Keaton was to perform the wedding of his son that Saturday. He was among the first to get out when flights resumed. He made it to the wedding with about thirty minutes to spare!

The World

firefighters, and health officials were aided by many rescue volunteers from outside the city.

This shocking and horrifying attack on America shattered the citizens' illusions of safety and security. For days, eyes were riveted to televisions, and phone lines were jammed as people tried to connect with family and friends across the country.

As investigations began to determine the backgrounds of the perpetrators, many American citizens of Middle Eastern background became victims of harassment by neighbors and others, including law enforcers. In some areas, mosques were vandalized.

New security procedures for travel went into effect, the likes of which Americans had never seen before.

2002 In May, Bobby Frank Cherry was convicted in the 1963 bombing of Sixteenth Street Baptist Church in Birmingham, Alabama.

2003 After months of anticipation, the United States launched a war against Iraq in March. In Operation Iraqi Freedom, armed forces invaded Iraq and took control of Baghdad, beginning efforts to end the regime of Iraqi leader Saddam Hussein. Although President George W. Bush declared an end to the major combat in May, fighting continues through press time.

The United Methodist Church

United Methodist churches across the connection opened their doors for prayer and for worship services. For the first few months after the attack, attendance in many churches increased. Unfortunately, within the year attendance had returned to pre-9/11 levels in most places.

2003 Elections for General Conference and Jurisdictional Conference delegates were held across the connection.

A change in the General Board of Pensions and Health Benefits policies resulted in a mass of early retirements of general agency staff, pastors, and conference staff. General agencies were particularly

The World

In a special ceremony on October 3, the remains of approximately 419 enslaved African Americans were reburied in New York City. Housed in carved mahogany coffins, the remains were carried in a procession to the African Burial Ground Memorial Site. These remains had been unearthed in 1991 when construction on a federal building in Manhattan commenced. What construction workers found is believed to have been the largest cemetery for enslaved African Americans in America, covering approximately six acres. It was believed that as many as 20,000 Blacks may have been buried there from colonial times. Archaeology teams and other scientists have been studying the remains and artifacts that have been housed at Howard University. Scholars and historians will no doubt find a gold mine of information about slavery and life in general in New York during colonial times.

The United Methodist Church

affected as thousands of years of experience left. Shortly after this time, more downsizing took place in some agencies.

Dr. Myron F. McCoy, senior pastor of St. Mark United Methodist Church in Chicago, Illinois, was named president of St. Paul School of Theology. He became the first African American to head a United Methodist-related seminary other than Gammon, a historically black seminary. Dr. McCoy had pastored St. Mark for eleven years. Prior to that he served as a district superintendent. Dr. McCoy was the last of many people mentored into ordained ministry by the late Rev. Dr. Maceo D. Pembroke. Dr. McCoy also headed the Northern Illinois delegation to the 2004 General Conference.

In an unprecedented action, the General Commission on the Status and Role of Women fired their two General Secretaries, both ethnic women. One was an Asian and the other an African American. While not much information was shared publicly, many in the church wondered how the agency charged with the monitoring of the church for justice for women could abruptly dismiss two executive women who had been employed barely a year.

In January 2004, M. Garlinda Burton, a distinguished journalist and author, was named Interim General Secretary of the General Commission on the Status and Role of Women, the top executive position. Burton, a highly respected laywoman, is known for her justice views. She was previously the editor of *Interpreter* magazine.

The United Methodist Church

"The Great Event" took place in Atlanta, Georgia, bringing together Congregation Resource Centers and Partner Congregations in a major learning and training event. Sponsored by the Coordinating Committee of Strengthening the Black Church for the 21st Century, the event was the culmination of the quadrennium cycle. Teams from Partner Congregations had an opportunity to receive learnings and resources from teaching teams from the Congregation Resource Centers. Worship, Bible study, and networking were integral components of the event.

Bishop Jonathan D. Keaton, chair of the committee, convened and presided over the event. Carolyn Johnson, vice president, facilitated the program. Cheryl Stevenson was the staff coordinator. Some of the program participants were Rev. Walter Kimbrough, pastor of Cascade United Methodist Church in Atlanta, Georgia; Rev. Tyrone Gordon, pastor of St. Luke Community United Methodist Church in Dallas, Texas; Rev. Alfreda Wiggins, pastor of Wesley United Methodist Church in Baltimore, Maryland; and Rev. Lillian Smith, General Board of Higher Education and Ministry. Marilyn Magee Talbert led Bible study. Rev. Joseph Daniels, pastor of Emory United Methodist Church in Washington, DC, and Henry Stewart, a young adult lay member of the Coordinating Committee, led a session on planning. Teams from Congregation Resource Centers led other workshop experiences.

Marilyn Magee Talbert was presented a commemorative plaque and gift for her two quadrennia of service to the Coordinating Committee.

The United Methodist Church

In November, a leadership summit on the state of the black church was called by the Ebony Bishops. In a historic action by the African American bishops of the church, several leaders across the church were invited to talk about the issues confronting the black church and about some possible remediation strategies. Dr. Trudie Reed, president of Philander Smith College, was the facilitator of the process. Dr. Reed served as a member of the Secretariat for the General Commission on the Status and Role of Women from 1977 to 1984, and later as Associate General Secretary of the General Council on Ministries. Erin Hawkins, staff member of the General Commission on Religion and Race, was the staff person and chair of facilities arrangements for the summit.

Word spread about the summit, and over two hundred fifty people from across the country attended. This attendance was indicative of the concern and the hope that leaders in local congregations and conferences were feeling about the black church.

Bishop Rhymes Moncure, convener of the Ebony Bishops group, and Bishop Gregory Palmer were the program designers. Bishop Felton E. May, host bishop, facilitated local arrangements. Other bishops in attendance were Bishop Melvin G. Talbert, retired, Ecumenical Officer for the Council of Bishops; Bishop James R. King, Kentucky Area; Bishop Charles Wesley Jordan, retired; Bishop Forrest C. Stith, retired; Bishop Alfred Johnson, New Jersey Area; Bishop Ernest Lyght, New York area.

2004

The General Conference convened in Pittsburgh, Pennsylvania, where the General Conference of The Methodist Church had met forty years earlier. The meeting forty years earlier was before The Methodist Church's union with The Evangelical United Brethren Church and during the time when The Methodist Church still maintained the "church within a church," the Central Jurisdiction.

One hundred forty-two African American delegates (including first alternates) were elected to the General Conference. Seven headed their delegations: Frank Beard, clergy, North Indiana; Myron McCoy, clergy, Northern Illinois; Cheryl Bell, clergy, Kansas West; Charlotte Abram, clergy, Nebraska; Robert E. Hayes, Jr., clergy, Texas; Joe May, clergy, Mississippi; James Swanson, clergy, South Georgia.

For the first time, Haitian Americans were identified as delegates to the General Conference. The two delegates, both from Florida, were Judith Pierre Okerson, a laywoman, and Jacques Pierre, a clergy male.

One of the features at the General Conference was a tribute to African Americans who had stayed in The Methodist Church (and predecessor bodies) in spite of segregation and racist treatment by the church. A video put together by the General Commission on Christian Unity and Interreligious Concerns showed pictures of many former and present leaders and a scroll of many living and deceased members who lived during those segregated times. This tribute was in response to the concern (and some anger) of some African American United Methodists about the repentance celebration held at the 2000 General Conference.

During the 2004 General Conference there were reports of ethnic participants not being recognized for opportunities to speak. When the issue was raised, the ignored people were further victimized by being "chastised" by Whites. For example, when one African American clergywoman was speaking, a white delegate asked an African American who the person was. When the black clergywoman finished, the white delegate got up and made disparaging remarks about her conference's failure to pay its apportionments in full. The remarks were irrelevant to the matters being discussed.

During the 2004 General Conference, a document surfaced calling for an "amicable separation" of the church over the issue of homosexuality. During a plenary session, Bruce Robbins, former General Secretary of the General Commission on Christian Unity and Interreligious Concerns, and Dr. Bill Hinson, president of the conservative Confessing Movement, spoke to the assembled conference. Dr. Robbins attempted to provide an explanation for the document. Although many assumed that Dr. Hinson was the author of the document, both he and Rev. James V. Heidinger II, president of the Good News Movement, said that was not true. In an interview for the *Daily Christian*

Advocate, Dr. Hinson said: "It was discussed, and my (Confessing Movement) leadership decided that (such a resolution) would be a very bad idea." The call for an "amicable separation" set up the call for a unity statement, which passed. Conversations in the halls and meeting rooms showed, however, that the church is anything but in unity.

Jurisdictional conferences met in July. Three African Americans were elected as bishops: Marcus Matthews in the Northeastern Jurisdiction, James Swanson in the Southeastern Jurisdiction, and Robert Hayes in the South Central Jurisdiction. Also in the Southeastern Jurisdiction was a hotly contested series of voting for another bishop. Arnetta Beverly, an African American district superintendent, maintained a steady level of support through a number of ballots, causing two white male challengers to finally withdraw. Then a white female challenger who had been a low vote-getter earlier in the process was finally elected on the thirty-fourth ballot, setting a voting record in that jurisdiction for the number of ballots required. Ironically, it was twenty years earlier that the Southeastern Jurisdiction refused to consider Bishop Leontyne Kelly a viable candidate. She was elected in the Western Jurisdiction, although Virginia was her home conference. Twenty years later the Southeastern Jurisdiction failed to elect a credentialed African American woman. Many reports of racist remarks came from participants in the jurisdictional conference. The jurisdiction remains a challenge for justice for those who are not white.

The United Methodist Church

The South Central Jurisdiction did not have an overt racist tone, but it too failed to elect a credentialed African American female district superintendent. It was reported that one delegation was adamant that they would not vote for any woman! The South Central Jurisdiction elected a female in 1992 and another in 1996.

It took sixteen years from Bishop Kelly's election before three more African American women were elected in 2000: Bishop Beverly Shamana in the Western Jurisdiction, Bishop Violet Fisher in the Northeastern Jurisdiction, and Bishop Linda Lee in North Central Jurisdiction. Thus the Southeastern Jurisdiction and the South Central Jurisdiction are now the only jurisdictions who have not elected an African American female.

The Board of Directors of Black Methodists for Church Renewal met with the New Interim Executive Director, Bishop Melvin G. Talbert, in Fort Lauderdale, Florida. Among the actions taken were to close the office at the General Council on Ministries building in Dayton, Ohio, and to open an interim office in Nashville, Tennessee. These actions were necessary because the General Conference dissolved the General Council on Ministries, replacing it with a structure called a Connectional Table, and decisions about use of the former GCOM building were not made at that time.

The Future Has a Past

Several months ago I embarked on a journey to discover the heritage of my faith and to put some of my discoveries into a format that people in local congregations can pick up and read, and through which they can find doorways to make discoveries of their own. I have learned much more than what this resource can contain. I have experienced an emotional roller coaster during this journey. I have felt pain, sadness, anger, and frustration at the indignities and injustices experienced by my ancestors. But there has also been pride, joy, and awe at the resilience, strength, and tenacity of people who were bold in their witness, who struggled to move forward, and who continued to forge paths for us to follow. They refused to allow circumstances and situations to define them. They knew that their current situation was not their final destination!

Yet, I am troubled by the current realities of our churches. Too many people in the pews are satisfied with a club mentality, not wanting to reach out with love to the hurting, the lost, and the least. Too many congregations long for the "good old days" that really were not all that good. We are in need of spiritual and visionary leaders. Leaders are not defined by their title—neither clergy nor laity—but by whether or not they can influence people to follow. Our need is for leaders who love people and who have a passion for ministry. Our churches can grow and be vital and vibrant beacons of hope. Churches that have become family chapels need to consider if they are maintaining an effective witness or whether they can become more effective through mergers, collaborations, and cooperative parishes. We need to recruit and develop pastors who have a commitment to the parish ministry and who will work and hone their craft of ministry. Laypeople need to know and understand the legacy they have inherited and strengthen their links of connection to the next generation. If the heritage of faith, the culture of the black church, and the memories of those who led the way and stayed are to survive, we have to understand that our future indeed has a past.

> Those that deny the struggles of their ancestors are not worthy of their accomplishments. And if you disown your past, you cannot be trusted with our future. Without our history some of us have nothing. And without our ancestors' history we are nothing.
> (From *The Real Rosewood*, by Lizzie PRB Jenkins. BookEnds Press, 2003.)

We entered this century with a lot of print, media, and technology focused on information and data analysis of the youth and young-adult populations. Diverse leaders can often spin the characteristics, wants, needs, likes, and dislikes of young people. The 2000 census offered insightful data about the African American population. While the picture presented by the census is not perfectly accurate, it offers legitimate trends well worth close attention. We are at a juncture where more than half of African Americans in this country are under the age of 30. African Americans are no longer the largest ethnic subgroup in America. The 2000 census included the new feature of multiracial identification, meaning that a person could check more than one racial group. People who are biracial claimed both parentages rather than defining themselves by one or the other. For the first time, African Americans who are offspring of Black-White, Black-Hispanic, or other combinations could and did define themselves as something other than American-born Blacks, as generations past had done. No longer did they have to adhere to the philosophy that "the touch of black blood makes one black." This possibility for acknowledging one's full heritage and background is a significant change and trend.

Findings from research other than census data yield other factors about young people. One study of young adults reports that the need for connection is common among today's young people. In regard to church, there are young people in the African American culture who

- are connected
- are not connected
- were once connected
- do not want to be connected

We also know that cross-racial adoptions are increasing among singles or couples who are not African Americans. Recent information tells us that women are outperforming men at various levels of society and that the number of women graduating from college is now higher than the number of men graduating from college, and the distance between the two numbers continues to grow.

Various data that examine and explore attitudes and perspectives of young people offer some insight, suggesting that young people today are not interested in history or dynamics of the past—whether those dynamics are historical, cultural, racial, or anything that happened the day before yesterday. Only the now is relevant. Young people are, however, more apt than their parents' generation to accept without prejudice the diversity and experiences of their counterparts. I suspect that the degree to which young African Americans are more accepting of their counterparts and less interested in the past is greater within The United Methodist Church than in other arenas.

And what are the dots to be connected from the aforementioned? Perhaps the most significant realization we can draw from the data is that there is a growing disconnect between our young people and the establishment of our United Methodist congregations.

In a recent consultation with young adults, I had the privilege of engaging some of the brightest and finest of our denomination. Many voiced their frustrations with our church, but for the most part they were willing to hang in there while advocating and working toward changes needed to draw in their peers. Yet these young adults were clear that there are many who are not willing to hang around and wait for opportunities to serve and to use their gifts. They are sick of hearing reasons that we did not make things better faster.

As this resource and other historical data indicate, African Americans are the only group in America that did not come here of their own free will. This group endured hundreds of years of slavery and legalized segregation; yet we have survived. There are volumes that extol how our ancestors did that. However, what needs to be shared with our young is that nothing in the past will guarantee success or failure. What I saw around that recent consultation table were young adults who will serve our church well, provided that we open ourselves up and create a more hospitable environment that will enable us to keep them. They have a lot to offer. What I would want the young adults to understand is that they are links that hold together what has passed and what is yet to come. Each generation must decide for itself whether it will choose to grow to the potential of its heritage or will be the generation to fail to move the legacy forward.

For the first time in our history there are more African Americans born after the era of the civil rights struggle than before. If our young do not pick up the baton and run the race before them, it will not be long before the African Americans in The United Methodist Church will decline at a fairly rapid rate. Too many of our congregations are beyond the

crossroads because of their refusal to change. Why sit here until we die? is a question that needs to be asked and answered.

On the other hand, a people who refuse to know anything about their heritage have no place in the future. We have this heritage, this culture, this faith that binds us. Come, let us walk together. I am convinced that the same God who brought the children of Israel through the Exodus experience, this same God who enabled black people to endure the middle passages, this same God who soothed the scars of the lash, this same God who enabled our people to bear burdens in the heat of hatred and of the day, this same God has not left us nor forsaken us. This same God continues to bless us, continues to hold us up in spite of racism even within the church; this same God will see us through. This mighty and awesome God we serve is waiting for us to come to ourselves, avail ourselves of God's power, and become the people of God, worthy of the legacy of faith entrusted to us. God is expecting something of us! In the words of one of my former pastors, Bishop James R. King, "God's will for us is good. We must do the rest."

Helpful Resources

BOOKS/BOOKLETS

African American Desk Reference, Schomberg Center for Research in Black Culture (New York: Stonesong Press, 1999).

Africana: The Encyclopedia of the African and African American Experience, Kwame Anthony Appiah and Henry Louis Gates, Jr., editors (New York: Basic Civitas Books, 1999).

Atlas of African-American History, by James Ciment (New York: Checkmark Books, 2001).

Before the Mayflower: A History of the Negro in America 1619–1964, by Lerone Bennett, Jr., revised edition (Chicago: Johnson Publishing Company, 1964).

Begrimed and Black: Christian Traditions on Blacks and Blackness, by Robert E. Hood (Minneapolis: Fortress Press, 1994).

Black Church in the African American Experience, The, by C. Eric Lincoln and Lawrence H. Mamiya (Durham: Duke University Press, 1990).

Black Firsts: 2000 Years of Extraordinary Achievement, by Jessie Carney Smith (Detroit: Visible Ink Press, 1994).

Black History, Monarch College Outlines (New York: Simon and Schuster, 1971).

Black Manifesto: Religion, Racism, and Reparations, Robert S. Lecky and H. Elliott Wright, editors (New York: Sheed and Ward, 1969). Out of print.

Black People in The Methodist Church: Whither Thou Goest? by William B. McClain (Cambridge: Schenkman Publishing Company, 1984).

Breaking Barriers: An African American Family & the Methodist Story, by Angella P. Current (Nashville: Abingdon Press, 2001).

Complete Idiot's Guide to African American History, The, by Melba J. Duncan (Indianapolis: Alpha Books, 2003).

Contemporary Journey: A Brief History of United Methodists in Ohio, by Frederick A. Norwood (A Bicentennial of American Methodism Publication, 1984).

Dark Glory: A Picture of the Church Among Negroes in the Rural South, by Harry V. Richardson (New York: Friendship Press, 1947).

Development of Negro Religion, The, by Ruby F. Johnston (New York: Philosophical Library, 1954).

Ethnic Minorities in The United Methodist Church, Ethnic Ministries—Board of Discipleship (Nashville: Discipleship Resources, 1976).

Forty Years in the Lap of Methodism: History of Lexington Conference of Methodist Episcopal Church, by Walter H. Riley (Louisville: Mayes Printing Company, 1915). Out of print.

Garden of American Methodism: The Delmarva Peninsula, 1769–1820, by William Henry Williams (Wilmington: Scholarly Resources, 1984).

Great African-American Women, by Darryl Lyman (New York: Jonathan David Publishers, Inc., 1999).

Heritage & Hope: The African-American Presence in United Methodism, Grant S. Shockley, General Editor (Nashville: Abingdon Press, 1991).

History of Lexington Conference, by D. E. Skelton (1950). Out of print.

In Black America, by Patricia W. Romero (New York: Books, Inc., 1969.) Out of print.

Journey, The: United Methodist Women in North Georgia 1878–1983, Centennial Celebration History Project Committee, Mrs. Marie W. Copher and Mrs. Lavinia B. Morgan, co-chairpersons (North Georgia Conference United Methodist Women, 1984).

Methodism and the Shaping of American Culture, Nathan O. Hatch and John H.Wigger, editors (Nashville: Kingswood Books, 2001).

Methodism's Racial Dilemma: The Story of the Central Jurisdiction, by James S. Thomas (Nashville: Abingdon Press, 1992).

Methodists and the Crucible of Race 1930–1975, by Peter C. Murray (Columbia: University of Missouri Press, 2004).

Mighty Like a River: The Black Church and Social Reform, by Andrew Billingsley (New York: Oxford University Press, 1999).

Negro Church in America, The, by E. Franklin Frazier (New York: Schocken Books, 1963).

Negro in the History of Methodism, The, by J. Beverly F. Shaw (Nashville: The Parthenon Press, 1954). Out of print.

Negro Segregation in The Methodist Church, by Dwight W. Culver (New Haven: Yale University Press, 1953).

Our Time Under God Is Now: Reflections on Black Methodists for Church Renewal, Woodie W. White, General Editor (Nashville: Abingdon Press, 1993).

Story of American Methodism, The: A History of the United Methodists and Their Relations, by Frederick A. Norwood (Nashville: Abingdon Press, 1974.

This Far by Faith: Stories From the African American Religious Experience, by Juan Williams and Quinton Dixie (New York: HarperCollins, 2003).

To a Higher Glory: The Growth and Development of Black Women Organized for Mission in The Methodist Church 1940–1968 (Education and Cultivation Division, General Board of Global Ministries). Out of print.

Trouble in Mind: Black Southerners in the Age of Jim Crow, by Leon F. Litwack (New York: Knopf, 1998).

Turning Corners: Reflections of African Americans in The United Methodist Church From 1961–1993, by George M. Daniels (General Council on Ministries, The United Methodist Church, 1996). Out of print.

Two Centuries of Methodist Concern: Bondage, Freedom and Education of Black People, by James P. Brawley (New York: Vantage Press, 1974). Out of print.

We Kept Them Flying, by David H. Hinton (Professional Press, 1998). Out of print.

With Unveiled Face: Centennial Reflections on Women and Men in the Community of the Church, by Theressa Hoover (New York: Women's Division, General Board of Global Ministries, 1983). Out of print.

Witnessing & Testifying: Black Women, Religion, and Civil Rights, by Rosetta E. Ross (Minneapolis: Fortress Press, 2003).

PERIODICALS/PAMPHLETS

American Legacy: The Magazine of African American History and Culture (New York).

Black Methodists for Church Renewal at The General Conference of The United Methodist Church, 1972 (Found in Garrett-Evangelical Theological Seminary Library, Evanston, Illinois).

Christian Social Action magazine (Washington, DC: General Board of Church and Society of The United Methodist Church).

Daily Christian Advocate of The General Conference of The United Methodist Church.

Ebony magazine (Chicago: Johnson Publishing Company).

Essence magazine (New York: Essence Communications Partners).

Jet magazine (Chicago: Johnson Publishing Company).

Lexington Conference Journals.

Report to the General Conference, 1972, United Methodist Church Commission on Religion and Race (Found in Garrett-Evangelical Theological Seminary Library, Evanston, Illinois).

UNPUBLISHED DOCUMENTS

Black Church Growth Consultation Report (August 25–28, 1988).

Findings of Black Methodists for Church Renewal, Board of Missions (Atlanta: 1970).

Future Directions, Black Methodists for Church Renewal (Dayton: 1988).

Affirmbration 15, an epigrammatic compendium on the commemoration of the fifteen-year celebration of Chicago Black Methodists for Church Renewal, by Dr. Philip A. Harley (1984).

PERSONAL INTERVIEWS

Dr. Jack Seymore, Dean, Garrett-Evangelical Theological Seminary, Evanston, Illinois.

Lina McCord, former director, Black College Fund.

Betty Henderson, former president and former executive director, National Black Methodists for Church Renewal.

Helen Ammons, retired Director of Student Services, Garrett-Evangelical Theological Seminary.

Bishop Melvin G. Talbert, bishop of The United Methodist Church, retired; first General Secretary, General Board of Discipleship of The United Methodist Church.